Karen Leigh Davis

The Exotic Shorthair Cat

Everything about Acquisition, Care,
Nutrition, Behavior, Health Care, and Breeding

With 42 Color Photographs

Illustrations by David Wenzel

About the Author

Karen Leigh Davis, a professional member of the Cat Writers' Association, has a background in journalism and business writing. She has written a pet care column and numerous feature articles on cats and other companion animals for national and regional magazines and newspapers. As a freelance writer with more than 15 years of experience, she has conducted extensive research on animal-related topics with veterinarians, breeders, and other experts. Davis comes from a cat-loving family and has a lifetime of experience living in the company of cats. She has bred and shown Persians and Himalayans, but she finds all felines, purebred or mixed, domestic or wild, irresistibly charming and beautiful. She lives in Roanoke, Virginia, with four Persian cats.

Photo Credits

Chanan: inside back cover, pages 28, 73, 85; Donna Coss: back cover, pages 4, 12, 20, 24, 37, 57, 68, 69, 77, 96 top, 100; Larry Johnson: front cover, pages 25, 80, 88 top; Mark McCullough: inside front cover, pages 5, 8 top and bottom, 32, 33, 45, 52, 56, 76, 84 top and bottom, 85, 88 bottom, 89 top and bottom, 93, 96 bottom; Bob Schwartz: pages 9, 13, 16, 17, 36, 45, 64, 92.

All inquiries should be addressed to:
Barron's Educational Series, Inc.
250 Wireless Boulevard
Hauppauge, NY 11788

International Standard Book No. 0-8120-9822-6

Library of Congress Catalog Card No. 96-47263

Library of Congress Cataloging-in-Publication Data
Davis, Karen, 1953–
    The exotic shorthair cat : everything about acquisition, care, nutrition, behavior, health care, and breeding / Karen Leigh Davis.
        p.   cm.
    Includes bibliographical references (p.) and index.
    ISBN 0-8120-9822-6
    1. Exotic shorthair cat. I. Title.
SF449.E93D38   1997
   636.8′2—dc21   96-47263
                           CIP

Printed in Hong Kong

987654321

Contents

Understanding Exotic Shorthair Cats 6
Hybrid Origins 6
The Long and the Short of It 7
The Persian Cat, the Allowable
  Outcross 9
The Exotic Personality 10

Acquiring Your Exotic 11
Before You Buy 11
Finding a Breeder 16
When to Take Home a Kitten 17
Choosing a Healthy Exotic 17
The Sales Agreement 18
The Registration Form 18

Bringing Your Exotic Home 20
Preparing for the New Arrival 20
Hazards in the Home 25
Hazardous Plants 27
Introducing Your Exotic to Other
  Pets 27
Introducing Your Exotic to
  Children 28
Cats and Babies 29
Holiday Hazards 29
Indoor Versus Outdoor Cats 30
Leash Training 31
Pet Identification 31

Feeding Your Exotic 33
Life-Cycle Nutrition 33
Growth and Reproduction Formulas 33
Adult Maintenance 34
Types of Cat Food 34
Popular Versus Premium Brands 35
Diet and Urinary Tract Health 36
Deciphering a Cat Food Label 37
How Much and When to Feed 38
Milk and Water 39
Homemade Diets 39
Obesity 39
Foods to Avoid 40

Keeping Your Exotic Healthy 42
Conditions Common in Exotics 42
Choosing a Veterinarian 43
Signs of Trouble 43
Annual Check-ups 43
Feline Diseases 45
HOW-TO: Feline First Aid 46
Tooth and Gum Care 55
Medicating Your Exotic 56
Preventing Hair Balls 57
Vital Signs 58
Euthanasia and Pet Loss 58

**Understanding Exotic
  Behavior 59**
Exotic Body Language 59
Vocal Language 59
Your Exotic's Senses 60
Balance and the Righting Reflex 61
HOW-TO: Dealing with Elimination
  Problems 62
Hunting Habits 64
Territorial Marking 65

Grooming Your Exotic 67
Shedding 67
First Steps in Grooming 68
Combing and Brushing Methods 69
HOW-TO: Bathing Your Exotic 70
Trimming Claws 72

Showing Your Exotic 73
How Cat Shows Began 73
How a Cat Show Is Organized 74
New Breeds and Colors 75
Showing Longhaired Exotics 75
Entering Your First Show 76
Traveling with Your Exotic 77
Traveling by Air 78
Boarding Your Exotic 79

The Exotic Breed Standard 80
CFA Exotic Show Standard 80

Blue exotic shorthair.

Breeding Your Exotic 91
Hard to Breed 91
Getting Started as a Serious
  Breeder 91
Breeding Complications 92
Arranging Stud Service 92
The Feline Facts of Life 93
Basic Feline Genetics 95
Breeding Strategies 96

Raising and Selling Exotics 97
Preparing for Birth 97
Delivering Kittens 97
Trouble Signs 99
Kitten Development 99
A Breeder's Responsibility 100

Useful Addresses and Literature 101

Index 103

Acknowledgments

I wish to thank Mary Falcon, Project Editor, for her patient guidance and skillful editing; CFA Exotic Breed Council Secretary Barbara Sims for names and telephone numbers of important contacts; Johanna Leibfarth (Desmin Exotics) for furnishing background information, breed history, and photographs and for reading selected chapters for me; Sue Fraser (Lion House Cattery) for discussing breed attributes with me; Linda Abt and Irene Kachel, exotic breeders, for submitting photographs of their cats; Will Thompson, CFA All-Breed judge, for reviewing breed history and editing selected chapters; and James Richards, D.V.M., of the Cornell Feline Health Center for answering my questions about feline health.

Karen Leigh Davis
July 1996

Cream and white exotic shorthair.

Understanding Exotic Shorthair Cats

Hybrid Origins

The exotic shorthair cat is basically a Persian cat with a short coat. Although thick and plush, the exotic's shorter fur is much easier to care for than the Persian's long, silky coat. Often called the "lazy man's Persian," the lovable exotic possesses the Persian's peaceful personality with the bonus of a low-maintenance coat that doesn't demand the daily grooming a longhaired cat needs. Along with the short coat and quiet temperament, the exotic possesses the Persian's charming physical "type" characteristics: the short nose, round cheeks, massive head, and boxy build. The exotic's small, rounded ears and large, wide-set, rounded eyes also give it that same sweet-faced appearance so highly prized by Persian fanciers. This cherubic expression combined with the luxuriant feel of the dense, plush fur is why many admirers refer to the exotic as the "teddy bear" cat.

Despite the exotic's obvious assets, breeders did not set out to intentionally develop a shorthaired version of the Persian. On the contrary, the fact that the exotic shorthair even became a breed in its own right was really a quirk of cat fancy fate.

The story began in the late 1950s and early 1960s, when some breeders of American shorthair cats (which were called domestic shorthairs until their name was modified in 1965) started to mix Persians into their breeding programs to improve body type and to introduce the color silver into the bloodlines. This practice of deliberate hybridization caused American shorthair offspring from such crossbreedings to begin displaying some decidedly Persian conformation traits, including rounder heads, shorter noses, cobbier bodies, and softer hair. Cat show judges apparently liked the new look, because many of these cats performed well in the show ring and received coveted final wins.

Indeed, these hybrid offspring seemed to combine many of the best-loved traits of their forebears: the Persian's docile, affectionate temperament along with the American shorthair's playful, alert intelligence. With Persians as popular then as today, some breeders realized that a short-coated, easy-care version of the Persian would make an equally popular addition to the "cat fancy," a term applied to those interested in the breeding and showing of purebred cats. But purist breeders were understandably appalled at the changes taking place in their beloved American shorthairs. They felt that the purity of their pedigrees was at risk and wanted nothing more to do with the American/Persian hybrids. Steps were taken to disqualify cats with hybrid traits from competition, a ruling that stands today in the American shorthair show standard.

Exotics might have slipped into oblivion from the outset had it not been for the late Jane Martinke, who at that time was an American shorthair breeder and a widely known Cat Fanciers' Association (CFA) All-Breed judge. At a 1966 CFA Board of Directors meeting, Martinke proposed that these appealing shorthaired hybrids be classified as a new breed. Doing so, she reasoned, would appease the American shorthair people who wanted to keep their breed's standard intact. It would also offer a legitimate venue for the hybrid cats to receive the recognition they deserved. As a result of Martinke's efforts, CFA allowed breeders to transfer their American shorthair hybrids to this new breed classification and begin exhibiting them as exotic shorthairs in championship competition, beginning with the 1967 show season.

The first exotics to win major show recognition were silvers. In 1971, a shaded silver male named Silver Secret of Gay-O and a chinchilla silver male named Grayfire's Cheyenne were the first exotics to win grand champion titles. Today, the exotic appears in all of the colors and patterns recognized in the Persian, including the "pointed" pattern, which produces a cat with the appearance of a shorthaired Himalayan. According to CFA's registration totals, the exotic ranks as the fifth most popular breed in the United States.

Because the first representatives of the new breed were "exotic" shaded and chinchilla silvers, colors not known to exist in the American shorthair prior to that time, the breed was dubbed the exotic shorthair. In 1993, CFA dropped the "shorthair" tag and began calling the cats simply "exotics." Out of habit, however, many breeders still refer to them as exotic shorthairs, as do most other cat-registering associations. Many enthusiasts agree that the name

Two exotic shorthairs can produce a longhaired kitten, if both parents are "heterozygous," or carrying the recessive gene for a long coat.

never was an appropriate choice. From the beginning, the name caused confusion, because novices often mistook the term "exotic" to mean a wild cat, such as a cougar or bobcat. The term "shorthair" is a misnomer as well, and not only because the exotic breed standard calls for a dense, plush coat that is "medium in length." Because of their Persian ancestry, about half of all kittens born in exotic litters turn out to be longhaired cats, due to the fundamental genetic laws that govern the heredity of coat length.

The Long and the Short of It

A short coat results when a kitten inherits the gene for short hair length from one or both parents. This gene for a short coat is always dominant, while the gene for a long coat is always recessive. A kitten inherits one gene for coat length from each parent. The kitten that inherits a shorthair gene from one parent and a longhair gene from the other will be a shorthaired cat,

Because exotic shorthairs and Persians are closely related breeds, the exotic is often described as a short-coated Persian.

An American shorthair cat: The exotic shorthair cat is a hybrid breed that resulted when American shorthair breeders began crossing their cats with Persians to improve type.

even though it carries the "hidden" longhair gene. Due to the dominance of the shorthair gene, the gene for long hair is not expressed. To be born with long hair, a kitten must inherit two recessive genes for long hair, one from each parent (see Basic Feline Genetics, page 95). These principles apply in any breed.

A cat that possesses both long- and shorthair genes is said to be *heterozygous* for short hair. A cat that has only longhair genes or only shorthair genes is said to be *homozygous* for this trait. Persians, for example, are homozygous, because they must possess two longhair genes before the recessive longhair trait can be expressed. Consequently, Persians, when bred to other longhairs, can produce only longhaired offspring. Most exotics, on the other hand, are heterozygous, having inherited both shorthair genes from their shorthaired ancestors and longhair genes from their Persian forebears. When bred to other heterozygous cats, they can produce either long- or shorthaired kittens.

This creates quite a dilemma for exotic breeders, who must decide what to do with the predictable percentage of longhaired kittens born in exotic litters. Most are sold as pets, because, at this time, CFA, the world's largest registry of purebred cats, does not allow longhaired exotics to be shown in championship classes as either exotics or Persians, regardless of how good their quality. However, efforts have been underway for some time to change this policy, although the outcome remains uncertain. Many enthusiasts are in favor of CFA accepting the exotic as a new division of the Persian breed. This move would allow longhaired exotics to be shown as Persians, a reasonable decision, considering that the CFA standards for Persians and exotics are identical, except for the coat description. A longhaired exotic is visually indistinguishable from a Persian. The difference is that an exotic's pedigree lists shorthaired cats in its ancestry.

Should CFA decline to create a division of the Persian class for the exotic, another option would be to create two show divisions for exotics, one for shorthairs and the other for longhairs. Some other North American cat-registering associations have already adopted this practice.

The Persian Cat, the Allowable Outcross

To introduce shorthair genes into their exotic bloodlines, breeders initially were permitted to use any registered shorthaired breed, including Burmese, British shorthairs, and Russian blues, in addition to the American shorthairs. Some exotic pedigrees still reflect these original outcrosses. In 1987, CFA closed the exotic stud book to all shorthaired cats as outcross breeds. Today, the Persian remains the only allowable outcross. (The Himalayan is also an allowable outcross in associations that recognize the Himalayan as a separate breed,

The Himalayan color pattern consists of darker markings, called points, on the cat's face, ears, feet, and tail.

rather than as a division of the Persian breed.) Because the exotic is essentially a short-coated Persian, this book would be remiss without a brief discussion of the Persian cat.

The first longhairs introduced in Europe around the sixteenth century came from Turkey. They were called Angora cats after the region of Ankara, where they were found. But other longhaired cats that later came from Persia (modern-day Iran) became more highly prized for their attractive, longhaired coats. Although these cats had longer faces and looked much different from the Persian cats we know today, they were the forebears of our modern breed.

Today, Persians have a large, round head, a short nose, small, wide-set ears, short legs, and a stout, compact body described as "cobby." They appear in at least 80 colors, which are grouped by division for show purposes. These include solid colors, silvers and goldens, shaded and smokes, tabbies, particolors, bicolors, and Himalayan or colorpoint. *Particolor* is a broad term for a coat of two or more colors, such as a tortoiseshell, which is black with patches of red. A *bicolor* has a coat of two colors, one of which is white (see Exotic Colors, page 81).

The Himalayans or colorpoints were developed by breeding Siamese cats with Persians to combine the Persian's beautiful, long coat and other features with the Siamese's distinctive coat pattern, which has dark markings called "points." Some cat-registering associations classify Himalayans as a separate breed, while others regard them as Persians. Persians are well loved for their quiet, gentle dispositions, but their long, luxuriant coats can mat easily and require daily combing to maintain in pristine condition.

The Exotic Personality

Like their Persian cousins, exotics are sweet-tempered, laid-back, nonaggressive cats that generally get along well with other cats and with dogs. Their quiet, relaxed, passive nature makes them particularly well suited to apartment living. They seem perfectly content to sleep all day until their owner comes home from work to provide a lap for TV-time napping.

This does not mean, however, that exotics are all sleep and no play; quite the opposite is true. That dash of American shorthair in them makes them a little more active than Persians, some believe, but exotics, being very people-oriented cats, seem to prefer interactive play with their owners. So, be prepared for having your toes attacked beneath the bed covers when settling down to sleep at night!

Exotics crave and thrive on human companionship. They prefer to spend their time in those rooms where you spend yours. Loyal and loving, they tend to select one individual in the household as their favorite person and typically follow that person from room to room, just to see what's going on. They nearly always choose the favored person's lap over anyone else in the room but, of course, if that person isn't available at nap time, any lap will do in a pinch!

Some breeders say that coat color seems to influence temperament, although no formal scientific studies have been conducted to support this casual observation. For example, blues and creams are reportedly more laid back and easygoing, while the tabby colors are more frisky and energetic. Like all cats, exotics are clean, and their quiet, yet playful, nature makes them ideal house companions.

Acquiring Your Exotic

Before You Buy

Although unpedigreed "alley" cats make just as good companions as purebred felines, acquiring an exotic shorthair has some special advantages. Because a purebred has a recorded ancestry, certain qualities, such as temperament and appearance, are more predictable. But as you consider getting an exotic—or any cat—remember that your new relationship could last at least a decade or longer. For greatest compatibility, the cat you select as your long-term friend must suit your personality and lifestyle. Before you commit, know what you want in a cat companion. To help you decide, consider the following:

Show Cat or Pet?

Breeders price and sell exotic shorthairs according to whether they are show-quality, breeder-quality, or pet-quality. Cats in all three categories are purebred and fully registrable in the cat associations.

Show-quality exotics are the most expensive to buy, because their breeders think they are outstanding examples of the breed, based on the standard, and will perform well in the show ring. Few breeders will sell a "top-show" cat to a novice. But many will part with proven winners retired from breeding if you agree to spay or neuter and show the cat in alter classes. This is a good way to acquire a high-quality show cat without the hassle of owning an intact, breeding animal.

When shopping for an exotic, consider buying from a breeder who has a proven track record in the show ring. That way, you avoid the "backyard" breeders who care more about quick profits than about healthy bloodlines. When shopping for a show-quality cat, study pedigrees carefully. The more grand champion titles that appear in the first two or three generations of a kitten's ancestry, the better the chances that it, too, may become a winner. Although price varies greatly, depending on availability and geographical location, expect to pay from $800 to $1,200 or more for a show-quality exotic kitten. Less common colors tend to be more expensive, and a cat considered to be of top show-quality may cost as much as $3,500.

Breeder-quality exotics fail to meet the show standard in some small way, yet they possess enough good qualities, in addition to their excellent pedigree, to potentially produce outstanding offspring. Breeder-quality kittens typically sell for slightly less than their show-quality littermates. Expect to pay from $550 to $800 or more for a breeder-quality exotic.

Pet-quality exotics are the most affordable. Although some minor cosmetic flaw—or a less extreme flattened face—may make these cats unsuitable for show ring competition, they are still ideal household companions. The pet-quality designation in no way means that the cat is less healthy or less desirable to own. So, unless you intend to show or breed exotics, a pet-quality exotic is your smartest buy. Expect to pay $350 or more for a pet-quality exotic, depending on availability, color, and geographical location.

Depending on geographic location, a top-show quality cat like this beautiful black exotic, is harder to find and costs considerably more than a pet-quality purebred.

Responsible breeders usually sell their pet-quality kittens with a signed agreement that the new owner will spay or neuter. To ensure that the agreement is honored, the seller may withhold the kitten's "papers," or registration slip, until the buyer furnishes a veterinary statement proving that the required operation has been performed. In this way, breeders aim to discourage unethical people from buying purebred cats at pet prices, breeding them for profit, and adding to an already overcrowded pet population.

One Cat or Two?

If you're away at work all day, consider getting two kittens so they can keep each other company while you're gone. If you cannot afford to buy two purebreds, think about adopting the second kitten from your local animal shelter. Mixed-breed cats make excellent pets as well as suitable companions for exotics. If you intend to show, remember, too, that mixed-breeds and part-exotics can be exhibited at many cat shows in the household pet category. In this category, cats are judged according to their beauty, condition and personality, rather than the breed standard. If your budget and living accommodations allow it, acquiring two kittens will double your pleasure.

Kitten or Adult Cat?

Most people understandably do not want to miss the cute kitten stage. However, acquiring a grown cat has some cost-effective benefits if it already has been altered and is up-to-date on its vaccinations. Adult cats often cost less than kittens, too, particularly if you find one that is being retired early from a breeding program or from the show ring, and the owner or breeder simply wants to find a good home for it. Although kittenhood holds special joys for cat lovers, it can be the most destructive stage. Kittens are not born knowing how you expect them to behave in your home. They have to be properly socialized and patiently taught not to climb your draperies and not to sharpen their claws on your couch. On the other hand, many adult cats are given up for adoption because of behavior problems related to their past care or lack of training. Sometimes all you have to rely on in such a case is the seller's word and reputation, so ask questions and do your homework! Find out as much as you can about an adult cat's history and health records before you buy.

Friends' and/or Family Allergies

As you consider getting a cat, think about the people close to you who no longer may feel comfortable visiting your home because their asthma or allergies worsen around cats. You don't want to acquire a cat, only to have to give it up later because your social or family life suffers. Proteins produced by the cat's salivary and sebaceous glands trigger the allergic response. These proteins are deposited on the cat's fur during grooming, then dry and flake into easily inhaled particles. The tiny airborne particles settle primarily in carpets, draperies, upholstered furniture, mattresses, walls, and ceilings.

For the person who experiences only mild or intermittent allergy symptoms, certain compromises may allow a comfortable coexistence with cats. Suggested coping strategies include vacuuming frequently, replacing carpets with hard floors, replacing upholstered furniture with vinyl or leather, washing the cat in distilled water once a month, applying anti-allergy wipes or sprays to the cat's fur, using an air purifier in the home, and keeping ductwork, furnace, and air-conditioning filters clean. Allergy medications and desensitizing allergy shots help in many cases. A new vaccine, currently undergoing clinical trials, may soon provide the most effective relief yet for people allergic to cats.

Male Versus Female

Both male and female exotics make equally fine companions when altered. If you are not going to breed cats, you definitely will want to alter your exotic when it reaches the appropriate age. To determine whether a kitten is a male or a female, raise the tail and look at the rear end. In the female, the genital opening looks like a small slit and appears directly below the anus. In the male, the anus and penis are spaced farther apart, and both openings are round.

Veterinarians have traditionally recommended that males be

Buying an adult exotic that has been retired early from breeding or the show ring is a more cost-effective way to acquire a nice purebred than purchasing a kitten.

neutered between eight and ten months of age and that females be spayed at six months. To ensure that indiscriminate breeding does not happen, however, some breeders elect to spay or neuter their pet-quality kittens early, *before* they sell them. This practice is becoming much more accepted, as studies have shown that early spaying and neutering appears to be safe and does not adversely affect feline maturity, as once thought. Generally, early spaying takes place between 12 and 14 weeks; early neutering is done between 10 and 12 weeks.

Spaying costs more, because the operation involves opening the abdomen to remove the ovaries, tubes, and uterus. Neutering the male is a somewhat simpler procedure that involves removing the testicles. Remember, however, that the one-time cost of spaying is still considerably less than the long-term cost of raising and finding homes for successive litters of kittens. If cost concerns you, ask your breeder, veterinarian, or local

Sexing kittens: In females (right), the genital opening appears as a small slit just below the anus. In males (left), the genital opening is round, with more space between it and the anus.

mates, making it a nicer pet and improving its chances of living a longer, healthier life. Animals that roam in search of mates are more likely to be killed by cars, injured in fights, or exposed to contagious diseases. Repeated veterinary bills for cats injured while roaming and fighting can quickly exceed the one-time cost of spaying or neutering. Spaying eliminates the female's bothersome heat periods along with her ability to become pregnant. The operation also eliminates the possibility of any disease or infections in the organs removed and decreases the chance of breast cancer occurring later in life. Neutering the male reduces aggressive behaviors, eliminates testicular diseases, and decreases the chance of prostate cancer later in life, as well as diseases in other glands affected by male hormones. Neutering also helps curb a male cat's tendency to spray urine in the house to mark his territory. Contrary to popular myth, your exotic will not grow fat and lazy after being spayed or neutered, unless you overfeed it. As in people, obesity in cats is caused primarily by too much food and too little exercise.

animal shelter about low-cost spay and neuter programs available in your area.

Benefits of spaying or neutering: Both operations reduce an animal's natural desire to roam in search of

Controlling pet overpopulation: Aside from the health and behavior benefits, spaying or neutering your pet exotic is simply the right thing to do in the interest of controlling the pet population surplus. About 75 percent of cats taken into United States shelters are euthanized each year, with annual figures fluctuating from a staggering 4.3 million to nearly 9.5 million since 1985. Countless others fall victim to the hazards of life in the wild. Because there simply aren't enough homes to go around for so many cats, responsible cat owners and breeders make it their moral duty to help control this tragic surplus by having pets altered and by not allowing intact cats to roam freely and breed indiscriminately.

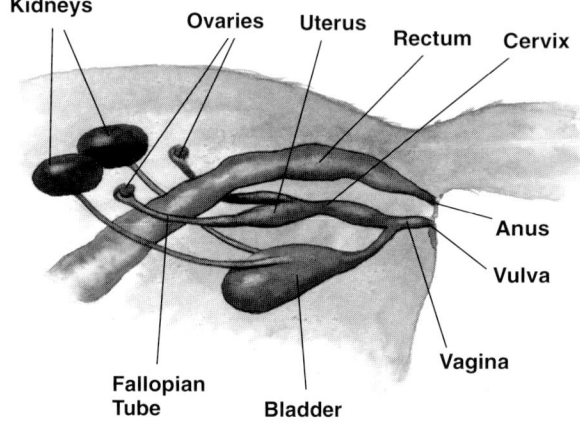

Kidneys — Ovaries — Uterus — Rectum — Cervix — Anus — Vulva — Vagina — Fallopian Tube — Bladder

Spaying removes a female cat's ovaries, tubes, and uterus so that she cannot have kittens.

14

Other Considerations

After you've decided whether you want a male or female exotic, show cat or pet, one cat or two, kitten or adult, consider several other important points:

Your lifestyle: Acquiring any cat demands a commitment on your part to take care of the animal's needs from kittenhood through old age. Cats can live an average 10 to 15 years; many have lived 20 years or more. So, look ahead into your own future and ask yourself if you'll be willing and able to provide your exotic with shelter, food, and regular veterinary care for a decade or two. Of course, it's impossible to predict the future, but if, for example, you realistically anticipate getting a job promotion that might require you to move across country within the next few years, it may be wise to postpone acquiring an exotic, unless, of course, you intend to take the cat with you when you move.

Housing situation: Make sure, too, that your housing situation is suitable for owning a pet. In some situations, certain restrictions may apply to, or even prohibit, the keeping of animals. If you rent, your landlord may require a pet damage deposit, in case your cat claws the drapes or carpets. This practice is neither uncommon nor unreasonable. As a cat owner, be aware that you are liable and responsible for any property damage or personal injuries your cat may cause. To avoid hassles, find out what rules and ordinances apply in your area. Then, assess your ability to fully comply, before you acquire a exotic.

Travel and time away from home: Animals need attention, so consider how much time you normally spend away from home. If you travel often, do you have a trusted friend or relative who is willing to

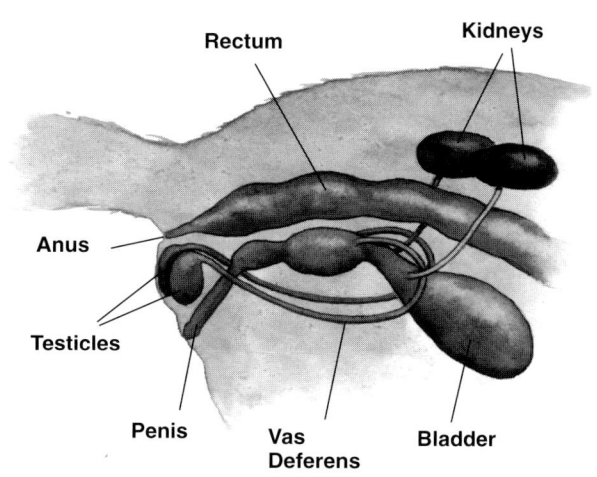

Neutering a male cat reduces or eliminates undesirable spraying behaviors and decreases the chance of prostate cancer later in life.

care for your exotic while you're away? If not, can you afford the frequent expense of boarding facilities and pet-sitting services in your area? Are you home enough to spend quality time with your cat and give it the love and attention it needs and deserves?

Your age and health: Certainly, most people expect to outlive their pets, but this is not guaranteed. Consider what would happen to your exotic if you died suddenly or became incapacitated by an injury or illness. Too often, an animal faces neglect, abuse, or abandonment if the owner hasn't planned ahead for its care in case of an emergency. This seems especially true in the case of pet owners who live alone. If you live alone, give a trusted person advance instructions—and keys—to enter your property immediately and assume care of your exotic if you die or become disabled.

An exotic kitten is adorable and irresistible, but before buying one, make sure you are willing and able to care for it for as long as it lives.

Finding a Breeder

If you've decided to buy an exotic shorthair from a breeder, the next step is finding a reputable one. Attending cat shows is the best way to meet breeders and see the quality of their cats. Cat fanciers' magazines list upcoming cat shows and publish breeder directories. The cat-registering associations also can refer you to breeders in or near your area (see Useful Addresses and Literature, page 101). Some breeders advertise in the classified sections of newspapers and trade magazines or pin their business cards on bulletin boards at veterinarians' offices. Talk with Persian breeders as well, since some breed both Persians and exotics. You want to find a conscientious breeder who is committed to improving the exotic breed's aesthetic qualities in terms of genetics, temperament, and appearance. This kind of breeder is typically involved in showing exotics as well as in breeding them.

Once you find a breeder, expect to put your name on a waiting list for a shorthaired exotic. This is because only about half of the kittens in exotic litters are born with short hair. In addition, most people who raise them have only a few litters each year. But even if you have to wait, small-volume breeders are still a good source to buy from because:

• You can see what one or both of the kitten's parents look like.
• You can see the environment where the kitten was raised.
• You can usually see other cats from the same bloodline.
• You can establish a relationship with someone who has experience raising and showing your chosen breed.

Questions a Breeder May Ask

When you first talk to breeders, you can gauge how much they care about their exotics by the kind of questions

Pets and wills: Make provisions for your cat in your will. In 1994, the Association of the Bar of the City of New York published an informative brochure titled "Providing for Your Pets in the Event of Your Death or Hospitalization" (see Useful Addresses and Literature, page 102). The pamphlet, among the first of its kind, simplifies the legalities involved and recommends that you will your cat outright to a friend or relative who has agreed in advance to comply with your wishes regarding its care. In your will, appoint that person as your cat's guardian. You also may wish to bequeath a modest sum of money to that person to cover the cost of your cat's care during its remaining years. For more information about wills and the laws in your state, consult a lawyer.

they ask you. For example, you've found a responsible breeder if he or she asks you about other cats you've owned, what you fed them, how often you took them to the vet, whether you kept them indoors or let them go outside, and what ultimately happened to them. You've found a conscientious breeder if he or she asks you what other pets you now own, why you want an exotic for a pet, and whether you intend to spay or neuter. Rest assured that such questions are not intended to make you feel intimidated or defensive. Instead, breeders who question prospective buyers this closely clearly care more about what kind of home their kittens will go to than about how much money they will make on the sale. They are likely to be equally conscientious about their kittens' health care and proper socialization.

A healthy, well-socialized kitten will have bright, clear eyes and an alert, friendly expression on its face. It should appear playful and relaxed around strangers.

Questions You Should Ask a Breeder

You should ask breeders what vaccinations the kitten has received, what cat association(s) they register with, and whether their cats are free from feline leukemia virus (FeLV) and feline immunodeficiency virus (FIV). Find out how much human handling the kitten has been accustomed to. Experts believe that kittens that are gently handled a little each day from about age three weeks on grow up to be more people-oriented and better socialized than those that have little or no human contact at all. If possible, visit the cattery and note its overall cleanliness. If the cattery is too far away for you to visit, ask to see pictures of the kitten and its sire and dam. Also, ask for references and talk to other people who have bought cats from the breeder.

When to Take Home a Kitten

A responsible breeder also will not let you take home an exotic kitten until it is at least 12 to 16 weeks old. By this time, a kitten has been weaned and litter trained, is eating solid food, and has had most or all of its vaccinations. Kittens taken away from their original surroundings too young sometimes suffer from stress and have trouble adjusting to a new environment.

In addition, if your kitten must be shipped to you, three to four months conforms with most airline age requirements. The breeder usually helps with shipping arrangements, but you can expect to pay all costs, including the airline-approved carrier the kitten will be shipped in. Costs vary, of course, depending on the airline and on the flight distance.

Choosing a Healthy Exotic

Once you've found a breeder, the kitten you select should have good muscle tone, bright, clear eyes, and an alert, playful personality. A healthy kitten should not sneeze or show mucus discharge around the eyes or nose. The ears should be clean and free of dark, crusty wax; head-shaking or ear-scratching may indicate ear mites or other infections. The anus should be clean and free of any signs of diarrhea. (Also, see page 42, Conditions Common in Exotics.)

The kitten's coat and environment should be clean and free of fleas. To inspect the coat for fleas, rub your hand against the fur and look for fine grains of black dirt, which is really flea excrement. Flea signs are more prevalent behind the ears, on the back, and at the tail base, where the kitten cannot easily reach to lick clean.

Tempt the kitten with a feather or ribbon and see how playful and relaxed it is around strangers. If it appears fearful, hisses at you, cringes from your hand or, in general, seems unused to being handled, look elsewhere for a better socialized kitten.

The Sales Agreement

A written sales contract describes all terms of the sale, including the purchase price and payment schedule, the breeder's health guarantee and any neuter/spay agreement. Contracts vary from breeder to breeder, of course, but all agreements should spell out the buyer's option to return the kitten and get his or her money back if the kitten is found to be unhealthy or unsuitable within a specified period after purchase.

The breeder's contract also may require the kitten's new owner to give the breeder the first option to buy back the kitten, if the new owner can no longer keep it. Some may even include provisions against declawing the cat or selling it to a pet shop. Monetary damages may be awarded if the breeder later learns that the buyer has violated any part of the agreement. Make sure you read and fully understand all terms of the contract before you sign.

Health records and vaccination certificates should accompany the sales agreement. To save money, some breeders vaccinate their own kittens, which is a legal practice. However, in areas where rabies shots are required for cats, the vaccine usually must be administered in the presence of a state authority, such as a veterinarian or an animal control officer, before a legal certificate can be issued. When shipping kittens by air, health and rabies certificates often are required, depending on the destination and on the airline's regulations.

In addition to health certificates, the purchase price should include the kitten's papers and pedigree. However, if the cat is pet-quality, the sales agreement may stipulate that the animal not be used for breeding. Under such terms, the breeder may rightfully withhold the registration papers until the buyer furnishes proof that the cat has been spayed or neutered (see page 100).

The Registration Form

Registering a kitten enables you to show it in purebred competition classes, if you choose to do so. Whether you intend to show or not, you want to buy an exotic that is registrable. This means that the kitten's pedigree, or family history, can be verified and accepted by a cat-registering association. An exotic without papers may not be purebred; after all, you have no proof of its parentage. On the other hand, it's important to understand that papers do not guarantee the health or quality of the kitten.

Depending on the terms of your agreement, the breeder may give you the kitten's registration slip at the time of sale or send it to you later. When you receive the form, simply fill it out with the name you have chosen for your exotic, complete the owner information section, and mail the form with the proper fee to the association(s) in which the breeder registered your kitten's litter. The breeder will have completed the sections on your kitten's breed, sex, hair length, eye color, coat color, etc. Also, if the breeder has a cattery name, it will be printed on the line where you write in the name you choose for your kitten. The cattery name will be part of your kitten's official, registered name. Most forms direct you to select two or three names, in case your first-choice name already has been used by someone else. When the association receives

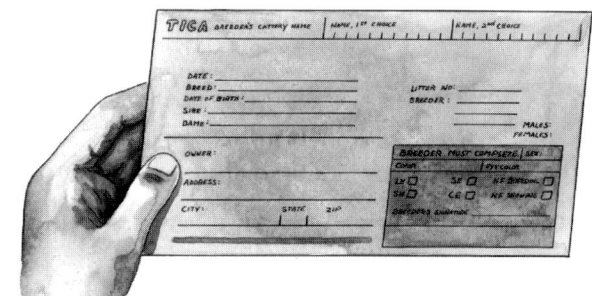

Registration papers document that your exotic comes from purebred ancestors; however, a breeder may rightfully wait to send you the registration form until after your pet quality kitten has been spayed or neutered.

the form, it will verify the pedigree information, approve your name selection, then send you back an owner's certificate.

Bringing Your Exotic Home

Preparing for the New Arrival

A little planning and preparation will make your exotic's transition to its new home much easier for all involved, particularly if you have children and other pets. Before you bring home the new arrival, go shopping and pick up some cat food and basic pet supplies to make your exotic's arrival as comfortable as possible. Following are some items you'll need:

Cat carrier: Purchase a suitable cat carrier for your kitten to travel in. Available at pet supply stores, and sometimes veterinarians' offices, carriers range from the inexpensive cardboard variety to the sturdier plastic ones, the wicker baskets, and the

If you don't want your exotic to sleep on your bed, keep your bedroom door shut, and give the cat its own bed or basket to sleep in.

canvas totebag varieties. If shipping your exotic by air, choose an airline-approved pet carrier. Regardless of the carrier type you select, it should close securely and be well-ventilated.

Furthermore, each cat in the household needs its own carrier for safe transport to the veterinary clinic or boarding facility. Never put two cats together in a single carrier, even if they are best friends. The too-tight quarters might cause them to fight.

Feeding dishes: Provide your new arrival, as well as every pet in the household, with its own feeding dish. If other pets try to eat the newcomer's food, feed the kitten in a separate area.

Stainless steel or glass dishes, although more expensive than plastic pet bowls, can be sterilized in the dishwasher without melting or warping. Some cats are allergy-sensitive to chemicals in plastic dishes and may develop itchy bald spots and crusty sores around the mouth and nose. Ceramic dishes come in decorative varieties, but select only those sold for human use or labeled as lead-free. Otherwise, you have no way of knowing whether the paint and glaze used on the dish contain harmful lead that may leach into your cat's food or water.

Exotics, with their flat faces and snub noses, seem to prefer flat, shallow saucers to deep bowls. Many cats don't like their sensitive whiskers to rub the sides of the dish as they eat. Some cats dislike this unpleasant sensation so much that they will resort to scooping out food morsels with their paws and eating off the floor. Also, select dishes that are heavy enough not to slide across the floor as the cat eats. Always wash feeding bowls after meals, and replenish water daily. In hot weather, exotics love a few ice cubes added to their water as a cool treat.

Litter boxes: To avoid litter box problems, provide one litter box per cat in your household. For a kitten's shorter legs, start with a shallow litter pan, then switch to a larger size as the cat grows. By the time your exotic is old enough to go to its new home, it already should know how to use a litter box. The instinctive digging and covering behaviors come naturally to cats. All you should have to do is show the kitten where its new litter box is. This is best done following the first meal or two in its new home.

Pet stores and mail-order catalogs carry a wide variety of litter pans, from the basic open plastic models to the fancy ones with ventilated bottoms and pull-out trays. The more expensive ventilated designs allow air to circulate beneath a litter tray to help dry the urine. Covered litter pans help contain odors and give shy cats privacy, but some cats seem to dislike the confinement. Regardless of the kind you select, it's important to keep the box clean, or the cat may stop using it if it becomes too soiled.

You'll also need a litter scoop to remove solid wastes from the box daily. At least once a week, clean the box with hot water and refill with fresh litter. A box of baking soda added to the litter helps control odor. Or try one of the many cat box odor control products available at pet supply stores.

For privacy, place the litter box in a quiet, undisturbed area of the house. Do not place it too near the cat's food dishes or sleeping quarters as cats normally do not like to eat or sleep near the place where they relieve themselves.

To prepare for your new kitten's arrival, you should buy a cat scratching post or a carpeted cat tree, a cat carrier, a cat bed, kitten food, feeding dishes, assorted cat toys, a litter box, a bag of kitty litter, a litter scoop, and some grooming supplies.

Kitty litter: Litter selection is important, because if your cat doesn't like the texture or scent of the type you choose, it may refuse to use the box. Some cats dislike the perfumed or chemically treated pellets added to commercial litters for odor control. These additives may please human noses, but cats seem to prefer their own scent. For really finicky felines, plain, untreated clay litter or sterilized sand may be better choices. Avoid using dirt from the yard or garden, however, as it may contain unwanted organisms, including the one that causes toxoplasmosis (see page 29).

Some litter brands are designed to clump when moistened, making it easy to scoop out urine along with solid wastes. This aids in sanitation and odor control by leaving behind only clean, fresh litter. For greater economy, certain litter brands can be rinsed

Cats have a natural need to sharpen their claws. To prevent your exotic from using your furniture for this purpose, provide a sturdy scratching post tall enough to allow a grown cat to stretch to its full length. To entice a cat to use the post, try rubbing some dried catnip leaves on it.

Carpet-covered cat trees give indoor cats a place to climb and sharpen their claws. Your exotic is more likely to use one if you install it in the room where you spend most of your time.

and reused. "Trackless" litter varieties are designed to stick less to cats' paws, reducing the number of granules tracked outside the box onto carpets and floors.

Grooming supplies: Buy nail clippers, steel combs, and a natural bristle brush. For kittens, start grooming with small and medium-size steel combs, and save a wide-toothed one for use on adult cats. For flea control, purchase a fine-toothed comb. Once caught in the comb's closely spaced teeth, fleas drown easily when dipped in a pan of water. A fine comb also readily removes flea dirt deep in the fur. Talcum or baby powder helps remove oil and dirt from a cat's coat when sprinkled in and brushed out completely. For bathing your exotic, select only pet shampoos labeled as safe for use on cats. Avoid dishwashing detergents, laundry soaps, or human shampoos. *Never* use dog shampoos or dog flea products on cats, because the ingredients may be too harsh and concentrated for felines. For tips on grooming your exotic, see pages 67–72.

Cat beds: More than likely, your exotic will prefer to sleep on your bed or in your favorite chair. Most cats like to snuggle in "cat cozies" made of soft, plush fabrics. Whether you buy a fancy pet bed or simply provide a blanket, select something washable, because you want to be able to clean your cat's bedding frequently.

Scratching posts: Cats, even declawed ones, have an instinctive need to scratch and sharpen their claws on objects in their territory. This natural behavior not only removes dead nail and reconditions the claws but also marks territory with scent from glands in the paw pads. The scent draws the cat back to the same scratching spot time after time. Obviously, this can pose a problem if your exotic starts clawing your furniture. To help avoid this problem, provide your cat with an alternative scratching post. Pet shops sell carpet-covered varieties, or you may wish to build your own.

Before introducing your cat to its scratching post, make sure the post isn't wobbly and won't tip over as the cat claws it. If a flimsy, unstable post falls over and scares the cat, the cat may refuse to use it ever again. The post also needs to be tall enough to allow an adult-size cat to stretch upward on its hind legs to its full length.

Some cats prefer bare wood or tree bark to carpet- or sisal-covered scratching posts. Others prefer a flat, horizontal surface to a vertical, upright post. If your cat has a strong preference either way, it may reject the post you provide. So be prepared to experiment with different varieties.

Carpeted cat trees that extend from floor to ceiling make attractive scratching posts and come in all colors to match any room's decor. Creative designs incorporate built-in perches and peekaboo condos for cat-napping and offer exercise and climbing opportunities for indoor cats. Because exotics like to be near their people, you may have better success getting your cat to use a scratching post if you place it in a room where you spend most of your time.

At an early age, introduce your exotic to its scratching post. Simply show the cat the post, move its paws in a scratching motion, and praise lavishly when it does what you want. If necessary, rub some dried catnip on the post to entice your exotic. It should soon learn to restrict its clawing to the designated area. If the cat decides to try out your furniture, scold verbally by saying "No" in a loud, sharp tone. Or, squirt jets of clean water from a water pistol to startle the cat without harming it. Wait a few minutes, then carry the cat to its scratching post. Never, *never*

To break an undesirable clawing habit, you may have to temporarily make the problem area unattractive and inaccessible to the cat by covering it with a bedspread, plastic bubble wrap, or large sheets of aluminum foil.

Combined with a loud, verbal "No!" or other negative command, squirting a cat with a jet of clean water from a squirt bottle or water pistol is a safe and harmless way to teach your exotic the error of its ways when you catch it in the act of clawing your furniture.

Although cats are often depicted in art playing with yarn balls, such toys are unsafe because the string can easily be swallowed.

hit your cat with your hand, with a folded newspaper, or with any other object—such abusive action only makes a cat fear and distrust you.

If your cat continues to claw the furniture, cover the problem area temporarily with a loosely draped blanket, wrapping paper, plastic bubble wrap, or sheets of aluminum foil. To discourage undesirable scratching habits, the idea is to make the inappropriate surface unattractive to the cat while offering a more appealing, acceptable substitute.

Cat toys: Ping-pong balls, golf balls, tennis balls, paper grocery bags (avoid plastic bags because cats, like children, may suffocate in them), and a cardboard box with cut-out peep holes make inexpensive cat toys. When selecting toys, consider safety first. Choose only sturdy toys that won't disintegrate after the first few mock attacks. Remove tied-on bells, plastic eyes, button noses, and dangling strings that your cat could tear off and swallow or choke on during play. Never let your exotic play with small items that could be chewed or swal-

lowed easily, such as buttons, hair pins, rubber bands, wire bread-wrapper ties, paper clips, cellophane, or candy wrappers. Also, avoid yarn balls, threaded spools, or string of any kind. Supervise all access to fishing-pole-style toys that have feathers, sparklers, and tied-on lures. These interactive toys provide great exercise, but put them in a closet when you're not playing with your cat. Also, be careful of braided rugs or knitted afghans that might unravel if the cat plays with a loose end. Once a cat starts chewing and swallowing string or yarn, a considerable amount may amass in the digestive tract and cause life-threatening blockages or perforations. If you come home to find your cat with a piece of string hanging out of its mouth, *do not* attempt to pull it out. Doing so can cause a more serious, even fatal, injury, if the string has already wound its way into the intestinal tract. Seek veterinary help immediately. Surgery may be required to correct this condition, called "string enteritis."

Catnip: Pet stores offer an array of catnip mice, catnip sacks, and other catnip scented toys. A member of the mint family, catnip is a perennial herb you can grow indoors or outdoors for your cat's enjoyment. Some cats go wild over it, rolling ecstatically and rubbing their faces in the dried leaves or scented fabric. Afterward, they lie sprawled on their backs in a trancelike state, as if drunk, purring loudly and contentedly. The substance in the plant that causes this reaction is called *nepetalactone*. The effect wears off in a short time, and the herb is not believed to be addictive or harmful to domestic cats; however, not all cats care for catnip. Many lack the gene that makes them respond to the plant's intoxicating effects, and they show no marked reaction when exposed to it.

Window perches: These carpeted shelves that attach easily to win-

24

dowsills give indoor cats an eye to the outside world. Place a bird feeder or bird bath in view of the window, and your exotic will be entertained for hours, as if watching "cat TV."

To prevent falls and escapes, make sure all window screens lock in place and are sturdy, tight, and secure enough to withstand the cat's weight if it lunges at a fluttering insect on the outside. Veterinarians treat enough injured cats that fall or jump from upper-story windows to give the condition a name—*high-rise syndrome*.

Hazards in the Home

Cats don't have to drink poisons to get sick. They can ingest wax, bleach, detergents, and other toxic chemicals simply by brushing against dirty containers or walking through spills, then licking the substance off their paws and fur. With this in mind, take an inventory of all household chemicals and other potential hazards in your home that a climbing, exploring cat might have access to. Then, to make your home cat-safe, do the same things you would do to make it child-safe:

• Store detergents, solvents, mothballs, insect sprays, and all other household chemicals out of reach in securely closed cabinets.
• Screen fireplaces.
• Keep tight-fitting lids on all trash bins so that foraging cats won't get sick by spoiled foodstuffs or injured by discarded razor blades, broken glass, or jagged tin can edges.
• Keep toilet lids down so that kittens can't fall in and drown.
• Cover sump pumps.
• Remove poisonous plants (see list on page 27).
• Avoid using edible rodent and insect baits where your cat might get at them and be poisoned.
• Keep perfumes, cosmetics, nail polish removers, and all vitamins and

Help your exotic shorthair cat live a longer, healthier life by keeping it safely indoors.

medicines, including aspirin and acetaminophen (highly toxic to cats), tightly capped and put away.
• Before shutting the dryer door, look to make sure your cat hasn't jumped in unnoticed. This advice applies to the washer, refrigerator, and other appliances, too.
• Tuck electrical and telephone cords out of reach under mats or carpets, tack them down, or cover them with PVC piping. Coating cords with bitter apple, bitter lime (available at pet stores), raw onion juice, or hot pepper sauce also helps discourage chewing. Chewing on electrical cords can result in burns and electric shock. If this

A dryer's dark, warm interior can seem cozy to a cat, and many are killed or injured each year because their owners accidentally shut them in before use. Make sure your exotic doesn't jump in unnoticed. Always look and take a head count before you shut any appliance door.

ies. But if an inquisitive cat should leap up on the stove top when you're not looking, it can get burned by stepping on a hot burner or by sniffing a boiling saucepan or tea kettle.

• Remove or secure all breakable items on tables, shelves, and bookcases that an exploring cat might knock over.

• Put away pins, needles, and threads when not in use to prevent your exotic from accidentally swallowing them.

• Consider children's toys that could pose potential dangers to a cat. For example, indoor basketball hoops over trash cans may trap a curious kitten in the netting, causing accidental strangulation.

• Read lawn care product labels carefully before using. Some pesticides, weed killers, fungicides, and fertilizers pose hazards to pets that walk in treated grass, then lick the chemicals off their paws.

• Supervise pets around swimming pools and ponds. Although cats can swim, kittens, especially, can drown from exhaustion if they fall in and can't find a way to climb out.

• Replace your car's traditional antifreeze with a "safer antifreeze" brand. Hose down all fluid leaks and antifreeze spills in the driveway or garage immediately. Ethylene glycol, the prime ingredient in traditional antifreeze, is deadly poisonous to animals. As little as half a teaspoon can kill an adult cat. Safer antifreeze products on the market contain *propylene glycol*, which is significantly less toxic than ethylene glycol. In fact, propylene glycol is used as a preservative in some foods, alcoholic beverages, cosmetics, and pharmaceuticals.

• Be aware that cats allowed outdoors in winter often crawl up under car hoods to sleep, because the engines stay warm hours after use. To alert sleeping cats, cautious people bang on the hood or blow the horn before

happens, disconnect the current before touching the cat, or use a wooden broom handle to disengage the cat from the wire. Even if the cat appears to suffer only minor burns to the tongue and mouth, consult a veterinarian immediately. Complications from electric shock may not surface right away.

• Keep window and drapery cords tied up and out of reach, as a frolicking feline can become entangled and accidentally strangle itself.

• Unplug small appliances when not in use. The dangling cords from a coffee pot or hot iron left unattended present a tempting hazard to a playful cat.

• Supervise all kitchen activities. Fortunately, most exotics aren't avid jumpers, due to their short, stocky bod-

Hazardous Plants

Amaryllis	Daffodil	Ivy	Oleander
Asparagus fern	Daphne	Jack-in-the-pulpit	Periwinkle
Azalea	Datura	Jerusalem cherry	Peyote
Belladonna	Delphinium	Jimsonweed	Philodendron
Bird of paradise	Dieffenbachia	Larkspur	Poinsettia
Black locust	(Spotted dumb cane)	Lily of the valley	Pokeweed
Caladium	Elephant ear	Lupin	Potato
Castor bean	Foxglove	Marijuana	Rhododendron
Chinaberry	Fruit pits	Mistletoe	Rhubarb
Christmas cherry	Hemlock	Monkshood	Skunk cabbage
Christmas rose	Henbane	Moonseed	Spider mum
Chrysanthemum	Holly	Morning glory	Umbrella plant
Clematis	Honeysuckle	Mushrooms	Wild cherry
Creeping Charlie	Hydrangea	Nightshade	Wisteria
Crown of thorns	Iris	Nutmeg	Yew

starting the car. The fan blades and other engine parts can cause fatal injuries if an unsuspecting feline gets caught underneath. This is another good reason to keep your exotic safely indoors at all times.

Hazardous Plants

Although carnivorous by nature, cats enjoy snacking on greenery, apparently because the added roughage aids in digestion. Unfortunately, cats often indulge this occasional craving by nibbling on decorative houseplants and ornamental shrubs. While many plants are harmless to cats, others are deadly. Ingestion can cause a wide range of symptoms, including mouth irritation, drooling, vomiting, diarrhea, hallucinations, convulsions, lethargy, and coma. If your cat displays any unusual behavior after chewing on a plant, consult a veterinarian immediately.

To make your house and yard cat-safe, avoid the common toxic plants listed above.

The list is only a partial one; therefore, if you are unsure about a particular plant's toxicity, call your veterinarian. The National Animal Poison Control Information Center (see page 47) also offers a comprehensive list of plants toxic to cats.

Besides nibbling on the greenery, it's also quite natural for a cat to mistake the dirt-filled base of a large potted houseplant for a convenient litter box. Unless you like your plants fertilized in this manner, cover the dirt with wire mesh or decorative rock.

Introducing Your Exotic to Other Pets

If you already have an adult cat or a dog, bringing a new kitten into their "territory" must be managed carefully. Before exposing any newcomer to your resident cat(s), have it checked by a veterinarian and tested for disease, especially feline leukemia virus (FeLV) and feline immune deficiency virus (FIV). While awaiting the test results, keep the new arrival isolated from other pets, in a separate room or in a pen. This also allows time for the "house smell" to settle on the newcomer, which may help make the introductions less threatening. After a few days, remove the new cat from its separate quarters for awhile and let the resident pets go in and sniff the new scent. When the time seems right, allow the resident

Wide-set eyes give this lovely blue and white exotic shorthair a sweet-faced expression. The breed standard calls for eyes that are round and large, level and set wide apart.

don't be dismayed if it takes as long as a month for the animals to accept each other and settle down. Cats are territorial, and adding a newcomer means new boundaries must be set. In time, the tension usually disappears. However, cats, like people, are individuals, and occasionally two turn out to be simply incompatible. Some breeders will agree to buy back a kitten if things don't work out in the new home. Just in case, always make sure your sales contract clearly states the terms of a return agreement.

Introducing Your Exotic to Children

Children find kittens irresistible, but they have to be taught how to handle them properly. Not only can a child injure a fragile kitten, but an animal frightened or annoyed by a child's unintentional roughness may defend itself by scratching or biting the child. To avoid such mishaps, teach your child that pets are not animated toys, and supervise all physical contact between small children and pets. If the child pulls on a cat's tail or ears, remove his or her hand and show the child how to gently stroke the animal's fur. Explain that loud screams and sudden movements may frighten the cat. Show your child where cats like to be stroked most—under the chin, behind the ears, and on the neck and back. Explain that some cats do not like to be stroked on their stomachs and rumps, while others will tolerate it from people they know well and trust. Teach your child how to properly pick up and hold a cat.

Picking Up a Cat

The proper way to pick up a cat is to put one hand under the chest behind the forelegs and the other hand under the rump to support the rear legs and body. Cradle the cat in your arms against your chest. Your exotic

pets to see and sniff the newcomer, but supervise all contact for the first few weeks. Keep dogs on a leash during these first meetings so they won't chase and frighten the newcomer. Gradually increase the exposure until the pets seem to coexist peaceably.

If you have rabbits, guinea pigs, birds, or other small pets, it's possible to achieve harmony among different species as long as you provide secure, separate living quarters for all and supervise any direct contact. Never leave adult cats alone with uncaged birds and small animals of prey. Cover aquariums with a hood, so cats won't be tempted to go fishing or swimming.

Although it's usually easier to introduce a kitten, rather than a grown cat, into a home that already has a feline, will let you know when it wants down. Although mother cats carry their kittens by the scruff of the neck, this method can hurt an adult cat if not done properly and should be reserved for emergency restraint. Even then, care must be taken to fully support the cat's rear legs and body weight with the other hand. Letting it dangle can injure those neck and back muscles. Likewise, never lift a cat by its front paws.

Cats and Babies

You may have heard the "old wives' tales" about cats sucking milk from infants' mouths and smothering them. Well, it's wise not to allow your cat to have unsupervised access to an infant, not because there's any truth to the old wives' tales, but because screams, cries, or jerky movements made by the infant could frighten the cat and result in accidental scratching or biting. If necessary, install a screen door at the nursery entrance. Also, to keep cats out of the cradle, consider buying a mesh crib tent. Baby supply stores sell these as well as cat nets that cover playpens and strollers.

Sometimes a cat may urinate on a baby's bedding or other items, "marking" them as part of its territory. Spaying and neutering tend to curb marking behaviors (see page 65 for more information on territorial marking). To reduce accidental scratches, trim your cat's claws regularly. And keep your cat in good health and free of parasites to reduce any risk of disease transmission to your child. Contrary to what those old wives' tales imply, cats and babies can coexist peaceably as long as you use some common-sense precautions.

Toxoplasmosis deserves a mention here, because it's one of those scary reasons well-meaning people bring up to convince mothers-to-be that their cats must go before a new baby comes. If you're planning to have a baby, get the facts first from your obstetrician and veterinarian. Tests are available to detect the disease, which is caused by a protozoan. Studies indicate that most people already have a degree of immunity to the disease. But if a pregnant woman is exposed to it for the first time, birth defects can occur. Cats get the disease by eating infected birds, rodents, or raw meat. Afterward, they shed the eggs in their feces. Humans can get it by handling soil or litter contaminated by the feces of an infected cat, but the majority of cases in humans are traced to people eating undercooked meat.

If your exotic never roams outdoors, never hunts, and never eats anything except pre-packaged pet food, the chances of it having the disease are nearly nonexistent. To avoid exposure, cook your meats thoroughly and never feed your cat raw or undercooked meat. If you become pregnant, wear gloves when gardening and when cleaning the litter box. Better yet, delegate the latter chore to someone else. If you know the facts and observe sensible precautions, there's no need whatsoever to give up your cat if you're going to have a baby.

As a general health precaution, keep indoor litter boxes and pet feeding bowls out of a crawling child's range. And cover children's sandboxes when not in use, so that free-roaming cats won't mistake them for giant, outdoor litter boxes.

Holiday Hazards

Accidental poisonings are a particular hazard during the Christmas holidays. To keep your cat safe, avoid decorating with poinsettia, holly berries, and mistletoe, which can be toxic to cats. Chocolate also is toxic to cats, so never leave desserts and candy dishes exposed where your exotic might sample the goodies when you're not looking. Resist the temptation to offer your

Anchor a Christmas tree to the wall, ceiling, or a doorknob to prevent your exotic from toppling it over. Avoid using tinsel and breakable ornaments.

exotic holiday table scraps, because rich, highly seasoned foods can cause diarrhea and stomach upset. A few bits of cooked, unseasoned turkey at Thanksgiving is okay, but be sure to *remove all bones*, as these can get caught in your cat's throat and cause it to choke.

To prevent a curious, climbing cat from toppling a Christmas tree, anchor the tree to a wall or ceiling by tying it to a hook. Because baubles and bells on Christmas trees present an irresistible temptation to playful paws, use only unbreakable ornaments. Cats also love to eat the tinsel that dangles so alluringly from decorated trees. While not toxic, the string-like foil can cause serious intestinal obstructions when swallowed, so avoid using it. The same applies to angel hair, artificial snow, edible ornaments, and small plastic beads or berries that could be swallowed easily.

In addition, aspirin and some commercial chemicals used as preservatives in Christmas tree water can be lethal to cats that might drink from the tree base. Avoid these chemicals, or keep cats out of the decorated room. Keep electrical cords on holiday decorations covered or out of reach, and unplug the Christmas tree lights when not in use.

Sometimes, people pose the greatest hazard to pets at holiday time. If your party guests tend to overindulge in the Yuletide "spirits," stow your cat in a quiet, safe part of the house while you entertain. That way, no one will accidentally step on or stumble over your cat or, in a moment of poor judgment, be tempted to offer it potentially toxic party treats, such as alcohol.

Halloween is a dangerous time for cats allowed outdoors, especially black ones, because some fall victim to vicious pranks. Holiday or not, some people dislike cats so much that they may resort to deadly means to keep free-roaming ones out of their flower gardens and trash cans, which is reason enough to keep your exotic safely indoors at all times.

Indoor Versus Outdoor Cats

Some people insist on letting their cats roam freely because they believe that depriving cats of their outdoor freedom is cruel, but it's true that cats kept indoors live longer, healthier lives. Indoor cats are less likely to be exposed to diseases, plagued by parasites, hit by cars, attacked by dogs, bitten by wild animals, caught in wild animal traps, poisoned by pesticides, and harmed by cruel people. By keeping your exotic indoors, you will have fewer veterinary bills related to injuries from cat fights and similar mishaps. In addition, you will have peace of mind, knowing that your well-kept indoor cat has little chance of contracting a disease or parasite that could be transmitted to you or your family. As long as you provide love and attention, your exotic will be quite happy and well-adjusted living indoors. If you feel your exotic must experience the outdoors, supervise outings in the yard, build an outdoor exercise run, or install a cat flap that provides safe access to a screened-in porch. You also can teach your exotic to walk on a leash, but never tie your cat and leave it unattended, not even for a minute. Without supervision, it could accidentally strangle or hang itself.

Leash Training

If you exercise patience and perseverance, you can teach your exotic to walk on a leash, although it will never "heel" with precision by your side the way a trained dog does. Some cats take to walking on a leash better than others. Much depends on individual temperament. To begin, select an adjustable nylon or leather cat harness and a lightweight leash. Most pet supply stores and catalogs market "figure-eight" harnesses designed specifically to restrain cats so that they can't slip free and escape. Do *not* use a choker collar designed for dogs. Also, be warned that cats can easily slip out of dog harnesses, so avoid those as well.

To begin leash training, accustom the cat to the harness by putting it on when you're home to supervise. Let the cat drag the leash freely behind it, but don't leave the cat unattended while doing this, because it might get entangled or accidentally hang itself. When the cat seems used to wearing the equipment, pick up the leash and, using a pull toy for enticement, gently coax it along for short distances. Praise lavishly when it goes in the desired direction. Practice indoors until your exotic walks comfortably with you on a leash inside the house. Then, go outside for short walks in a quiet area. Until your cat adjusts to unfamiliar sights and sounds outdoors, take along a pet carrier so that, if something frightens the cat and causes it to struggle on the leash, you can simply pop it in the carrier for safety.

To allow your exotic to safely experience the outdoors, teach it to walk with you on a leash.

Pet Identification

Cats allowed outdoors sometimes stray too far from home and then can't find their way back. Even cats kept indoors occasionally escape and get lost in unfamiliar territory. For these reasons, and because some desperate people steal pets for sale to research laboratories, your cat is safer if it wears some sort of identification.

Tattooing: While tattooing won't prevent your cat from being lost or stolen, a permanent ID may enhance its chances of recovery. Many laboratories will not buy a tattooed animal, and most shelters look for tattoos. A painless procedure provided by many veterinarians, tattooing involves inking the owner's Social Security number or a special code on the rear inner thigh. For best results, register the tattoo with a nationwide pet protection service that has a 24-hour hotline for tracing the number and finding the owner, no matter where the cat is

Red tabby exotic shorthair.

found (see Useful Addresses and Literature, page 102).

Collars and tags: These can be lost or removed, but they are better than nothing. A cat collar needs to have a stretch elastic or a breakaway section, so the animal can escape without choking if the collar catches on some object.

Like collars, ear tags embedded in the ear like a tiny earring are better than no ID at all, but they, too, can be cut off, ear and all, by unscrupulous pet thieves.

Microchips: Animal shelters in many areas are using microchip technology to reunite lost pets with their owners. To use such an ID system, the owner has a veterinarian inject a tiny microchip under the skin between the cat's shoulder blades. The chip reflects radio waves emitted by a hand-held scanner that reads the chip's code number. The owner registers the code number in a computer database for tracking. Ask your veterinarian if this system is available in your area.

Feeding Your Exotic

Life-Cycle Nutrition

"Good" nutrition depends a great deal on a cat's age, activity level, and current state of health. What's good for a kitten is not necessarily the best choice for an older cat, and vice versa. In fact, research has shown that certain nutrients consumed at too high or too low levels during early life stages may contribute to health problems in later life. This knowledge ended the old "womb-to-tomb" practice of feeding cats one food their entire lives and ushered in a new era of "life-cycle nutrition." Today, life-cycle formulas scientifically tailored to meet a cat's nutritional needs during different stages of its life compete for grocery store shelf space. But with so many varieties to choose from, the important thing to remember is that no one perfect pet food exists for every cat and for every owner.

Although pet food labels provide helpful information, choosing a cat food solely by label contents or brand name is unwise. Instead, base your selection on how well your exotic performs and maintains its overall condition on a particular food. Start with high-quality foods your breeder or veterinarian recommends. Then, during annual check-ups, when your veterinarian assesses your exotic's condition, remember to ask about your cat's changing dietary needs as it grows and matures.

Make recommended changes to your cat's diet gradually, over a period of at least a week. Begin by mixing small amounts of the new food with its current rations. Gradually increase the amount of new food as you decrease the amount of old food until the changeover is complete.

Growth and Reproduction Formulas

Kittens: For its first full year, your exotic kitten needs a greater amount of high-quality protein for growth than it will require in adulthood. At least 30 to 40 percent of a kitten's diet should be protein. Select a kitten or feline growth formula designed to meet this extra need and follow the feeding guidelines on the package. Kittens require more frequent feedings, but in smaller quantities, than adult cats. Newly weaned kittens need three or four feedings a day. By age six months, two meals a day should suffice. Most dry kitten formulas come in smaller pellets, making it easier for tiny mouths to chew.

Ever alert for the sound of the refrigerator opening, exotic shorthairs have a hearty appetite and, unless overfed, are generally active enough to stay fit and trim, like this cream tabby exotic.

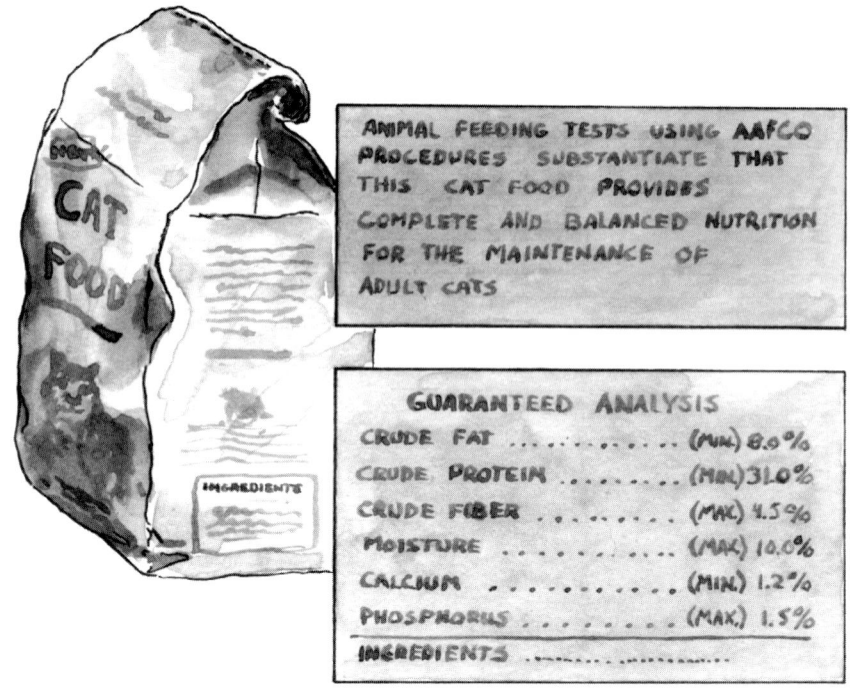

ANIMAL FEEDING TESTS USING AAFCO PROCEDURES SUBSTANTIATE THAT THIS CAT FOOD PROVIDES COMPLETE AND BALANCED NUTRITION FOR THE MAINTENANCE OF ADULT CATS

GUARANTEED ANALYSIS
CRUDE FAT .... (MIN) 8.0%
CRUDE PROTEIN .... (MIN) 31.0%
CRUDE FIBER .... (MAX) 4.5%
MOISTURE .... (MAX) 10.0%
CALCIUM .... (MIN) 1.2%
PHOSPHORUS .... (MAX) 1.5%
INGREDIENTS ....

Manufacturers substantiate claims that their cat food offers "complete and balanced" nutrition in one of two ways: chemical analysis or feeding trials. The method used is disclosed in the product's statement of nutritional adequacy. The required guaranteed analysis gives approximate, not exact, nutrient amounts in the can or bag.

Pregnant cats: Breeding females should also receive food formulated for feline growth and reproduction during periods of gestation and lactation. Because of the extra demand placed on their bodies, pregnant and nursing cats need more calories and high-quality protein to aid in fetal develop-ment and milk production.

Adult Maintenance

Moderately active cats: Adults need enough nutrients, fiber, and protein to satisfy their appetites, yet prevent them from getting fat, so choose a suitable food formulated for adult maintenance. Because adult maintenance formulas contain less protein than the growth and reproduction foods, they are unsuitable for growing kittens or pregnant cats, but

adequate for a normal, non-breeding adult's lower energy requirements.

Senior cats: Foods labeled "for all life stages" are designed to meet the needs of all cats, from kittens to senior citizens. However, older, less active cats often require fewer calories, less salt, and less protein than these diets contain. In addition, older cats com-monly require a food that is formulated for greater digestability. So, with your veterinarian's advice, consider an appropriate "senior" formula when your cat turns 10.

Types of Cat Food

Commercial pet foods come in three types: canned, dry, and semimoist (soft-dry). Generally, dry foods are less expensive and more convenient.

Canned foods contain more moisture than either dry or semimoist foods, making them a better choice for cats that need more water due to a medical condition. Because canned foods often contain more protein and fat, they are generally more palatable to the cat. Finicky eaters seem to like them better, although most will not touch food after it has been refrigerated. Most cats prefer their food served at room temperature. To avoid spoilage, take up the leftovers as soon as the cat finishes eating.

Dry foods help maintain better dental health, because the hard chewing action scours the teeth and gums. The recommended daily amount of dry food also can be left out all day in a bowl for cats to nibble free-choice, whereas canned foods spoil quickly. At one time, it was thought that nibbling on dry foods throughout the day predisposed cats to feline urologic syndrome (FUS) by allowing the urine pH to become too alkaline. But this is no longer the case. Today, most major cat food brands have been reformulated with acidifying ingredients to better maintain urine pH levels within normal acidic ranges. Offering proper portions free-choice is a recommended method for feeding dry food.

Soft-dry nuggets or semimoist foods attempt to combine some benefits of the dry and canned forms, making them attractive for the human consumer to use. Like dry rations, semimoist foods can be left out and fed free-choice without spoiling, and they do not have as much of an odor as canned foods. Unlike dry foods, semimoist products are too soft to help reduce dental tartar. At one time, these products contained a preservative called propylene glycol, which is the same chemical used in safer antifreeze brands. When this preservative was implicated in causing red blood cell damage in cats, responsible manufacturers removed it from their cat food products.

With so many choices available, it's easy to find a good product that your exotic enjoys and that is convenient for you to serve. Choose products guaranteed on the label to provide complete and balanced nutrition for your cat's current stage of life. To provide variety and appetite appeal, select two or three high-quality products your exotic seems to like and use them interchangeably. Well known for their finicky eating habits, cats have a discriminating sense of taste. Once developed, their taste preferences can be difficult to change. A cat fed the same food all its life may steadfastly refuse any sort of dietary change, even if its health depends on it. To avoid creating this finicky behavior, alternate a few varieties of cat foods and flavors from kittenhood on.

Popular Versus Premium Brands

Cat foods are marketed according to generic (economy brands), popular, and premium brands. While the cheaper generic foods, which are typically sold under a private label or store name, tend to be lower in quality and use poorer-grade ingredients, this is not always true. Sometimes it's cheaper for a manufacturer to simply stick a generic label on a popular brand and market it under a different name without changing the formula. The nationally advertised, popular name-brand products are sold in supermarkets, while the more expensive premium brands are sold primarily through pet supply stores and veterinarians' offices. Other than price, some popular and premium brands may differ very little. Although most premium brands tend to be more nutrient dense and more digestible, there is no regulated definition for what a "premium" product should be and no higher nutritional standard that a premium pet

Like people, cats get fat from too much food and too little exercise. Feed your exotic according to pet food package guidelines, and provide ample toys and carpeted climbing trees for play and exercise.

Diet and Urinary Tract Health

Over the years, numerous dietary elements have been blamed in the formation of struvite crystals that can plug the urethra in FUS, a potentially life-threatening disease. (Some veterinarians refer to FUS as LUTD or FLUTD, for "feline lower urinary tract disease," an umbrella term used to describe all disorders of the lower urinary tract.) The suspect list has included ash, magnesium, phosphorous, and calcium, among others. As each suspect ingredient was incriminated, major cat food manufacturers promptly reformulated their foods to reflect prevailing scientific and consumer concerns.

Current findings suggest that the overall mineral composition of cat food, rather than an excess of any single ingredient, determines whether the urine pH balance becomes too alkaline (too high), providing favorable conditions for crystals to form in the urinary tract. Magnesium content remains a secondary concern, enough to warrant restricting dietary levels when managing FUS. Reflecting this knowledge, specialty foods proliferate the market bearing label claims of "low magnesium," "reduces urinary pH," or "helps maintain urinary tract health." Beyond these permissible statements, cat food manufacturers cannot claim that their products treat or prevent FUS, or any disease, without approval from the Food and Drug Administration, because to do so would be touting the diet as a drug. These special diets, as well as many regular cat foods now on the market, contain enough acidifying ingredients to help keep urine pH within safely acidic ranges. An acid urine helps dissolve struvite crystals or prevents them from forming in the first place.

Researchers have noted a decrease in struvite stones along with an increase in similar stones composed of calcium oxalate. The obvious

food must adhere to. The word is simply a marketing tool. The general assumption is, however, that premium foods contain higher-quality ingredients and remain stable in their makeup, whereas popular brands are more likely to change recipe ingredients according to the current market cost and availability of those ingredients. It is also assumed that the product research behind premium brands is more substantial; however, many well-known popular brands are also backed by extensive research and years of experience on the part of the manufacturer.

Prescription diets also are available through veterinarians for cats with special needs due to heart disease, kidney disease, intestinal disorders, obesity, or other health problems. While most special diets come in dry or canned form, at least one for recurrent gastrointestinal problems is available in semimoist form.

conclusion is that the recomposition of commercial diets fed to cats is at least partly responsible for both changes. While studies clearly suggest that restricting magnesium and maintaining a slightly acidic urine may help prevent struvite-related urethral obstructions, such a diet is not a cure-all for *all* cats, particularly if it has the potential to cause other problems. What this means is that, while the link between diet and urinary tract disease remains under investigation, the best advice is to consult your veterinarian before starting your cat on any special diet.

Feeding a complete and balanced, high-quality commercial cat food formulated for your cat's life stage will help keep your pet robust and healthy looking, like this beautiful blue exotic.

Deciphering a Cat Food Label

Complete and Balanced: Pet food companies are required by law to supply certain nutritional information on their labels. To prove that their products comply with nutritional guidelines set forth by the Association of American Feed Control Officials (AAFCO), and to substantiate claims of "100% complete and balanced" nutrition, pet food manufacturers subject their formulas to chemical analyses or feeding trials. Feeding trials offer more assurance that food is adequately nutritious, because the product has been test fed to cats for a period of time under AAFCO protocols. Any product that has undergone feeding trials says so on the package. Look for the company's statement of nutritional adequacy, which should say something similar to: *"Animal feeding tests using AAFCO procedures substantiate that [this brand name] provides complete and balanced nutrition for the maintenance of adult cats."*

Guaranteed Analysis: The required "guaranteed analysis" must state on the label only whether minimum or maximum amounts of nutrients, in percentages, were met. The label doesn't have to list actual concentrations of specific nutrients. The problem with not knowing how much a product exceeds the minimum requirement for a certain nutrient, such as protein, is that sometimes too much can be just as bad as too little, depending on the cat's age and condition. What that means is that, while foods formulated for "all life stages of cats" are designed to meet normal nutritional needs of cats of all ages, some individuals, particularly older ones or those predisposed to certain health problems, may get far more of certain nutrients than they need.

Ingredients List: Ingredients are supposed to be listed in descending order of predominance by weight, but, this can be somewhat misleading. For example, meat may be listed first, leading the consumer to believe the product contains mostly meat, when in reality, the summation of separately listed grains and cereals makes plant material the predominant ingredient. Some labeling terms are strictly regulated, while others are not. For example, the title wording of "Chicken for Cats," "Chicken Platter," "Chicken Entree," etc., can have different meanings in terms of the percentage of chicken the product must contain. A good way to check specific ingredient amounts is simply to call the manufacturer's toll-free number on the package and ask for the data. Many companies have consulting veterinarians and/or nutritionists, and you can judge for yourself how willing and able they seem to be to share information and answer your questions. A manufacturer's long-standing reputation can offer some assurance that correct product standards are met and maintained.

Dry Weight Analysis: Because label percentages are based on the entire food formula, water and all, one must standardize the base of comparison when reading labels of dry, canned, and semimoist foods. This is done by calculating the "dry weight," the food content that would be left if all of the water were removed. First, determine the percentages of moisture and dry matter in the food. The guaranteed analysis already contains part of this information. If the label says the moisture content is 78 percent, subtract that figure from 100 percent (total food formula) to calculate the dry matter. In this case, the dry matter in the food is 22 percent.

Once you've calculated the dry matter, you can do a dry weight analysis for each nutrient in the food, based on the label guarantees. The formula for this is simple:

$$\frac{\% \text{ Nutrient}}{\% \text{ Dry Matter}}$$

For example, we've already determined that the dry matter is 22 percent; now we want to know how much of that matter is protein. The guaranteed analysis on the label says the food contains a minimum of 10 percent crude protein. (The word "crude" means the maximum or minimum

amount was determined by laboratory assay and not by feeding tests.) That 10 percent figure is based on the food's total formula, including moisture content; however, on a dry matter basis, the protein content is:

$$\frac{.10 \ (\% \text{ protein})}{.22 \ (\% \text{ dry matter})} = .45 \text{ or } 45 \text{ percent}$$

To support normal growth and reproduction, AAFCO recommends that at least 30 percent of a cat's diet be protein. For maintenance of adult cats, protein content should be at least 26 percent. These are recommended minimum amounts, based on dry matter, that foods should contain. In the above example, the label guarantees the product to be no less than 45 percent protein (dry weight basis), but it doesn't tell you whether the actual protein content exceeds that stated minimum. This information might be important if, for example, your cat requires a protein-reduced diet.

Although the dry weight analysis is a good way to compare nutrient percentages in different types of foods, it's not an exact measurement of daily nutrient intake. Remember, label guarantees are expressed either in minimum (not less than) or maximum (not more than) percentages, but not in actual amounts. If you're concerned about feeding too much or too little of a certain ingredient, consult your veterinarian. He or she can best judge your exotic's individual nutritional needs.

How Much and When to Feed

As a guide to daily rations, follow the feeding instructions on the package. Remember, however, that the amount of food your exotic requires each day will vary with its age, weight, and activity level. Adjust rations as necessary to maintain optimum body weight and condition. Generally speaking, a cat is at its optimum weight when you cannot see the ribs, but you can feel them without probing through thick layers of fat. Here again, your veterinarian can best judge your exotic's overall body condition.

Most adult cats thrive on two meals a day, morning and evening. Others do well on a canned food breakfast, combined with the measured daily amount of dry food left out for free-choice nibbling. Whatever routine works best for you and your cat, be sure to feed your exotic at the same time and in the same place each day.

Give each cat in the house its own food and water dishes. Establish your exotic's feeding place in a quiet location, where there is little noise and foot traffic, and stick to a regular feeding schedule.

Milk and Water

Keep fresh water in a clean bowl available for your exotic at all times. Cats can concentrate their urine and conserve water when necessary, but, like most other mammals, they cannot survive for very long periods without water.

Milk is not a substitute for water, nor is it a complete and balanced diet for adult cats. Some adult cats, like some people, develop a lactose intolerance to milk and will develop diarrhea if they drink it. Milk is useful as a temporary supplement for newly weaned kittens. When offering milk as a supplement, use a canned kitten milk replacer (available through veterinarians or pet shops) or a half-and-half mixture of evaporated milk and warm water. Avoid homogenized cow's milk.

Homemade Diets

Carnivores by nature, cats need protein from animal sources to stay healthy. They cannot adapt safely to a vegetarian diet. Nor can they thrive solely on "people food." Their nutritional needs are significantly different from those of humans, dogs, and other mammals; therefore, constructing a balanced meal for a cat from scratch is

best left to experts. Reputable pet food manufacturers budget substantial amounts of money for research to back claims that their products provide "complete and balanced" nutrition for feline life stages. Without expert guidance, the home-based chef cannot guarantee an adequate mix of proteins, carbohydrates, fats, vitamins, minerals, and amino acids essential to the feline diet.

One amino acid in particular, taurine, is indispensable, because the cat cannot manufacture this ingredient on its own. If its food is taurine deficient, a cat could develop blindness or cardiomyopathy (heart muscle disease).

Because the feline diet requires a delicate balance of numerous ingredients to maintain proper body functions and cell growth, too much or too little can be harmful. For this reason, home cooking should be attempted only in rare situations when a cat is suspected of being allergic to an ingredient common in commercially prepared foods. Even then, the makeup of any homemade feline diet requires close veterinary supervision.

Obesity

Obesity is probably the most common nutritional disorder among pets in

In general, a cat is too fat if you cannot feel its ribs without having to probe through thick, fleshy layers. Fat cats also often have sagging, pendulous bellies, bulges around the neck, and heavy accumulations of fat at the base of the tail.

the United States. Exotics, because of their passive, laid-back personalities, may be slightly more prone to this problem than some other breeds that are known to be more active. Cats that live in apartments and get little exercise also seem more prone to this disorder. As in humans, obesity in cats can pose some serious health risks. The extra weight puts a strain on all organ systems and contributes to a shortened life span. Also, an overweight cat is a greater surgical and anesthetic risk.

Like humans, cats become fat for the same reasons—too many calories and too little exercise. While many cats with free access to food self-regulate their consumption appropriately, others overeat out of boredom. Owners often unwittingly contribute to the problem by offering too many high-fat, high-calorie gourmet treats between meals.

Some overweight cases may result from feeding cats together, which encourages competition. In addition, many cats tend to gain weight as they grow older, simply because they play less and need fewer calories. Weight gain and weight loss also can be symptoms of serious underlying medical conditions, such as diabetes, thyroid disorders, and kidney disease; therefore, a veterinary examination is in order before you reduce your cat's feed or attempt to put it on any special diet.

Weight-Loss Diets

Your veterinarian can recommend an appropriate weight-loss method to suit your cat's particular situation. Some veterinarians prefer to use a good weight-reduction prescription diet, while others recommend continuing on the usual food, but cutting back the amount fed and eliminating treats. Prescription weight-reduction diets are nutritionally balanced but lower in calories to produce weight loss without creating other deficiencies. They are also higher in fiber to promote a feeling of fullness in the animal. If your veterinarian recommends a prescription diet, and you have more than one cat, you may have to feed the one on the special diet separately. Whatever method is used for any feline weight-loss program, owner compliance is the key to its success. And as with humans, gradual weight loss is more likely to result in long-term maintenance of the desired bodyweight.

Foods to Avoid

Dog foods are for dogs. Cat foods are for cats. Do not feed your exotic dog food, because dog chow does not contain nearly enough protein or taurine to promote good health in cats. If you have a dog and a cat, provide each with its correct food, and feed them in separate locations if they steal each other's food. Be aware of the following:

• Vitamin and mineral supplements, unless prescribed by a veterinarian, are not necessary when you feed your exotic a nutritionally complete and balanced commercial cat food. To compensate for nutrient losses during processing, pet food manufacturers add vitamins and minerals to their formulas to supplement natural nutrients contained in the primary ingredients.

• Table scraps do not provide a balanced diet, although they are okay as occasional treats. Garbage is garbage, so never feed your exotic scraps that you would not eat. Also, do not feed bones, as these may splinter and lodge in your cat's throat or puncture parts of the digestive tract.

• Do not feed raw meats, raw fish, raw liver, or raw egg whites. Meat alone is not a balanced meal and, if served raw, may contain harmful bacteria and parasites, including the organism that causes toxoplasmosis. Raw fish can cause a thiamine deficiency. Raw liver, if fed daily in large quantities, can cause vitamin A toxicity. Raw egg whites have an enzyme that can interfere with vitamin biotin absorption. An occasional egg yolk is okay, as long as it is cooked.

• Chocolate can be toxic to cats and dogs, so keep candies, desserts, and

Table scraps do not provide balanced nutrition for your exotic, although they are okay as an occasional treat. If you never offer scraps from the table, your exotic likely will never pick up the undesirable habit of begging at the table.

baking chocolate covered and out of reach. Alcohol is toxic to cats, even in small amounts—never let anyone give your cat alcohol. Some people think it's funny to watch a cat lap up a little beer, then see it stagger in drunken circles. This practice is cruel and dangerous, because a cat's smaller body mass cannot adequately absorb alcohol's toxic effects. Just a little "hair of the dog" can turn deadly and fatally affect an animal's breathing.

Keeping Your Exotic Healthy

Conditions Common in Exotics

Because of their outcrossings with the Persian breed, exotics share a vulnerability to certain conditions that their Persian relatives also are predisposed to. These include:

Excessive tearing: Because of their flat faces and short noses, exotics and Persians can have constricted tear ducts that do not always allow for proper drainage. The resulting discharge that accumulates at the eye corners needs to be wiped daily with a cotton ball and cleaned with a commercial tear stain remover. Some cats with greatly exaggerated *brachycephalic* (flat-faced) features may have a marked drainage deficiency, making them more prone to related sinus and eye infec-

Because of their flat faces and short noses, exotics are prone to develop tear stains in the corners of their eyes. Use a cotton ball to wipe the eye corners clean each day.

tions. Generally, cats with wide-spaced eyes experience fewer problems, while those with eyes set closer together, giving them a pinched look, tend to have the cramped tear ducts and nasal passages that promote chronic congestion. The wide-set eyes give the exotic its sweet-faced expression, so this attribute is not only more aesthetically pleasing in the breed, it is also more desirable from a health standpoint.

It's also important to note that, while the extreme flat-faced appearance is currently popular in show ring competition and, therefore, much sought after in show-quality exotics, pet-quality cats with less flattened facial features tend to pose fewer health problems for the average pet owner, who simply wants a nice companion animal to enjoy.

Closed or narrowed nostrils: The exotic's flat-faced appearance occasionally results in some undesirable facial deformities. One of these is called *stenotic nares*, which is an extreme narrowing or constriction of the nostrils. This, of course, interferes with normal breathing through the nose and forces the cat to breathe through the mouth. Before buying an exotic, look closely at the nostrils to make sure they are round and open and not pinched closed and compressed by the surrounding structures. Also, note whether the cat or kitten appears to breathe mostly through an open mouth and whether it sounds congested when forced to draw air through the nostrils.

Improper bite: One of the most common problems associated with the exotic's flat facial construction is called *malocclusion*, in which the upper and lower teeth and jaws do not properly align. If the problem is severe enough, it can interfere with the cat's ability to eat and chew its food properly. Before buying an exotic shorthair, open the mouth and examine the way the teeth come together. The flat surfaces of the upper and lower molars and incisors should meet evenly when the jaws close. The lower jaw should not protrude beyond the upper jaw.

Eye problems: The exotic's larger, more rounded eye surfaces predispose it to potential blunt trauma-type eye injuries. The upper and lower borders of the eyelids also tend to roll inwardly against the eyeball on occasion. This condition, called *entropion*, allows the facial hair to scratch the cornea, which can result in eye ulcers. The condition can be corrected surgically.

Reputable breeders take great care to cull unsound cats from their breeding programs so that their bloodlines remain healthy and free of genetic defects. Before buying any purebred kitten, it is always wise to talk to other people who have purchased cats from that breeder to determine what, if any, medical conditions have surfaced in the bloodlines.

Choosing a Veterinarian

Whether you choose someone in general veterinary practice or someone who treats cats exclusively, selecting a veterinarian for your exotic is one of the most important decisions you will make as a cat owner. Make sure you feel at ease with the way the veterinarian deals with you and your exotic. Does he or she seem interested in answering your questions? Does he or she thoroughly address your concerns and explain terms, procedures, and findings? Does he or she

show you how to administer medications? Does the clinic offer additional services, such as grooming and boarding, that you might use later? Establish a good rapport with your veterinarian and his or her staff, because their professional guidance will be a valuable asset to your ongoing education as a pet owner.

Important: Keep the clinic's emergency number handy, in case your exotic becomes ill or injured.

Signs of Trouble

Often, a sudden and persistent change in appetite is the first hint that all is not well with your exotic's health. Whether your exotic eats markedly more or less or stops eating altogether, any change in normal eating habits should be regarded with suspicion. Likewise, if you notice that your exotic is losing weight, drinking more water, vomiting frequently, experiencing diarrhea, straining to urinate, or urinating more often, schedule a visit to the veterinarian. Other trouble signs include coughing, sneezing, bleeding, staggering, swellings, panting, lethargy, lameness, coat changes, nasal discharge, bloody urine, bloody stool, crouching in a hunched-up position, hiding in unusual places, and breathing difficulty. This list is by no means complete. Because sick cats often seek seclusion, keep your exotic indoors and under close watch, and get veterinary help as soon as possible.

Annual Check-ups

Routine, preventive health care benefits both your cat's health and your pocketbook. The cost of treating a single serious illness can quickly surpass the money you spend on yearly physicals and annual booster shots throughout your exotic's lifetime. Even though keeping your exotic indoors minimizes its risk of contracting an illness from a free-roaming animal, several infectious

Ideal Vaccination Schedule*

Disease	1st Vaccination	2nd Vaccination	3rd Vaccination	Booster
Panleukopenia	6–8 weeks	10–12 weeks	16 weeks	yearly
Calicivirus	6–8 weeks	10–12 weeks	16 weeks	yearly
Rhinotracheitis	6–8 weeks	10–12 weeks	16 weeks	yearly
Chlamydiosis	6–8 weeks	10–12 weeks	16 weeks	yearly
Rabies	12–16 weeks	64–68 weeks		triannually
Leukemia	10–12 weeks	16 weeks		yearly

*NOTE: The age of the cat, type of vaccine, and route of administration influence the number of vaccinations required. Follow your veterinarian's recommendations.

diseases common in cats are caused by airborne organisms. This means a disease can waft into your home through open doors and windows or get tracked in on your shoes. Even your hands and clothing can serve as transmission modes. Fortunately, highly

The annual visit to your veterinarian is an important part of your exotic's health care routine. Keep all recommended vaccinations up to date.

effective vaccines exist to combat many diseases so, even though your exotic will remain inside, keep all vaccinations current.

Vaccines artificially induce active immunity by stimulating the production of antibodies against a specific organism. As long as the antibody level remains high enough in the body, the antibodies can attack and overcome a disease organism that attempts to invade. But because this protection wanes over time, your exotic needs annual booster shots throughout its lifetime to maintain an adequate level of antibody in the system.

The ideal vaccination schedule begins with giving a kitten its first combination shot for upper respiratory infections and feline distemper at approximately six to eight weeks of age. At about 10 to 12 weeks, another shot for upper respiratory infections and distemper is administered, along with the first in a series of two shots for feline leukemia virus (FeLV). At about 16 weeks, kittens get the works, with repeats of the previous vaccines, plus a rabies shot. A year later, all vaccinations given at 16 weeks are repeated and thereafter followed up with yearly boosters. A convenient, combination injection for cats is available now that provides one-year protection against feline leukemia virus (FeLV) and the upper respiratory diseases.

Kittens acquire maternal antibodies from their mother's first milk, the colostrum. How long this "passive immunity" lasts depends upon the antibody level in the mother's blood when the kittens are born. Protection usually lasts from 12 to 16 weeks, but it may wear off as early as eight weeks. Because kittens are highly susceptible to certain infectious diseases, vaccination at about eight weeks is recommended to ensure that they remain protected. However, if maternal antibodies are still present in the kitten's system when it receives its first shots, those passive antibodies may render the vaccines ineffective. That's why the shots are repeated at 12 and 16 weeks, to ensure that they "take," as well as to provide the kitten with continuous immunity as maternal antibodies wear off.

Feline Diseases

Feline Viral Rhinotracheitis (FVR)

Commonly called "rhino," this upper respiratory disease caused by a herpes virus makes an infected cat look and act like it has a common cold, with symptoms of sneezing, nasal discharge, and crusty, watering eyes. Often, the cat stops eating. Highly contagious, the disease spreads easily from cat to cat through direct contact with body secretions and contaminated objects, such as litter boxes, feeding bowls, or even human hands. Some cats show only mild symptoms and recover quickly, while others become progressively worse and may develop severe complications, such as eye ulcers. In some cases, the virus damages the throat, sinus and nasal structures, leaving the cat prone to repeated bacterial infections in those areas. Rhino has a high mortality rate among kittens and older cats. Many

Exotics with less exaggerated flat-faced features tend to have fewer problems with sinus and nasal congestion, from cramped nasal passages and blocked tear ducts.

cats that survive the acute illness become chronic carriers and, during stressful periods, will shed the herpes virus, making them a hazard to other cats in the household. By far the most effective way to reduce the occurrence and severity of upper respiratory infections is simply to vaccinate all cats.

Black exotic. Keeping your cat on a regular vaccination program, as recommended by your veterinarian, can help prevent most common feline illnesses.

Be Observant

Cats often conceal illness or pain, but observant owners can detect subtle behavior changes that cue them that all is not well. Early injury and disease detection can greatly enhance the odds of full recovery. Set aside time once a week to assess your cat's overall condition. Make a practice of inspecting your exotic for white teeth, pink gums, clean, pink ears, clear, bright eyes free of discharge, clean fur free of flea dirt, and a firm body free of lumps, bumps, and tender spots. By doing so regularly, you are more apt to notice anything out of the ordinary.

Be Prepared

Once recognized, the key to successfully coping with any emergency is to be prepared for it. Always keep your veterinarian's emergency number handy. In addition, assemble the following items in a first aid kit:

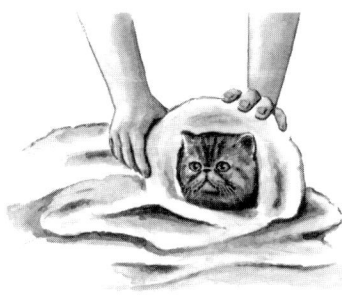

To safely restrain a struggling cat, wrap it in a towel or blanket, leaving only the head sticking out. Remember, an otherwise gentle cat may bite or claw you if it is frightened or in pain.

Be prepared for emergencies with basic first aid supplies. The most important item to keep handy is your veterinarian's emergency service telephone number.

• a blanket or towel to wrap your cat in for warmth and safe restraint
• gauze pads and strips for bandaging
• peroxide (it's fresh only if it bubbles) to clean wounds and induce vomiting
• syrup of ipecac to induce vomiting
• antibiotic ointment, such as Neosporin, for superficial wounds
• tweezers, handy for removing foreign objects from paw pads or from the throat, if the cat is choking
• ice pack for controlling swelling and bleeding
• scissors and adhesive tape
• artificial tears or sterile saline eye rinse to flush foreign material from eyes
• rectal thermometer, pediatric size

Control Bleeding First

If an injured cat loses too much blood, it may go into shock and die before you reach a veterinary clinic. To control bleeding, cover visible wounds with gauze pads or some clean material and apply gentle, direct pressure over the site for several minutes. Do not attempt to splint or straighten fractured limbs, as this could cause more damage.

Transport Properly

Never pick up an injured animal by placing your hands under the belly. This will only worsen chest or abdominal injuries. If the cat is lying down, approach it from behind, slide one hand under the chest and one hand under the rump, and gently place it in a pet carrier or on a blanket for transport. If the cat is crouched, grasp the scruff of the neck with one hand, place the other hand under the hips and rear legs for support, and cradle the cat in your arms. If the cat struggles, wrap it in a towel or blanket, leaving only the head sticking out.

Remember, no matter how gentle your cat, it may bite or claw you if it's in pain. Position an unconscious cat on its side for transport and cover it with a blanket to keep it warm.

Accidental Poisoning

If you suspect your cat has ingested a potentially hazardous substance, call your veterinarian immediately. Do not induce vomiting unless an expert advises it, as some substances can cause more harm when vomited back up. When advised to induce vomiting, administer a small amount of syrup of ipecac by mouth with an eyedropper. If this emetic is unavailable, peroxide or warm salt water usually works well. If the poisonous substance is known, take the package or a sample with you to the veterinarian.

For 24-hour assistance, seven days a week, call the National Animal Poison Control Information Center, operated by the University of Illinois. The hotline number is (800) 548-2423. The service charges a fee for each initial case, payable by credit card, but follow-ups are free. Those with short questions and those not wanting to use credit cards may have the

An easy way to avoid a potential emergency is to never *leave your cat unattended in a parked car on a warm day. Even with the windows cracked, temperatures inside the car can climb high enough to cause heat stroke and death.*

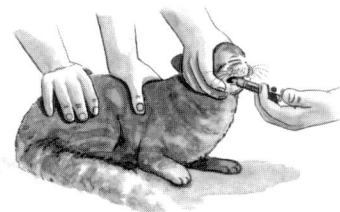

Induce vomiting only at the advice of your veterinarian or another expert. To administer a liquid emetic, tilt the cat's head back slightly, insert the tip of an eyedropper or syringe in the back corner of the cat's mouth, and slowly squeeze in a few drops at a time.

charge added to their telephone bill by calling (900) 680-0000.

Certain medications and flea control products cause some cats to salivate a little immediately after application. In many cases, this is no cause for concern, and the reaction subsides after a minute or two. However, if your cat begins salivating *heavily* after you've applied a topical flea preparation to its fur, or if it staggers or shows other unusual signs, rinse the substance off right away and call your veterinarian. Don't use the product on your cat again.

Similarly, if your cat's coat or paws become contaminated by bleach, pesticides, paint products, household cleaners and disinfectants, oil, tar, antifreeze, or other potential poisons, wash off the offending substance immediately. If necessary, clip away the affected fur. If the coat appears to be heavily saturated, or if you believe the cat may have already licked some of the substance from its coat or paws, seek veterinary help.

Removing Foreign Objects

If the cat is salivating, gagging and pawing at its mouth, it may be choking on a foreign object in its mouth. First, open

the mouth, attempt to pull out the tongue, if you can do so safely, and look down the throat. If you can see an obstructing object, use tweezers to gently extract it. If the object does not readily dislodge, make no further attempt to remove it without veterinary assistance. You may do more harm than good. Never poke tweezers into the eyes or ears; foreign objects here are best removed by a professional.

Heat Stroke, Frostbite

Heat stroke and frostbite require immediate medical attention. To prevent frostbite, keep your cat indoors and avoid overexposure during cold weather. To prevent heat stroke, never leave your cat in a parked car, not even for a few minutes, not even with the windows cracked. Temperatures inside a car climb too high for safe tolerance, even on mild days. With only hot air to breathe, your exotic can quickly suffer brain damage and die from heat stroke. Signs of heat stress include panting, vomiting, glazed eyes, rapid pulse, staggering, and red or purple tongue. Cool the body with tepid water, wrap in wet towels and transport to a veterinary clinic immediately.

Feline Calicivirus (FCV)

Like FVR, FCV is an upper respiratory infection with similar symptoms, except FCV is more likely to progress to pneumonia. Painful tongue and mouth ulcers can make the disease particularly disabling, as the cat may refuse to eat or drink. Muscle soreness, exhibited by a stiff gait or limping, also may be present. Some cats that recover from calicivirus become carriers.

Feline Pneumonitis

Also called feline chlamydiosis, pneumonitis is caused by an organism called *Chlamydia psittaci* that is neither a virus nor a bacterium. Like FVR and FCV, pneumonitis begins with weepy eyes and swollen eyelids. The disease is extremely contagious, especially in kittens. Again, the best defense is vaccination.

Feline Panleukopenia Virus (FPV)

Sometimes called feline infectious enteritis, feline parvovirus, and feline distemper, FPV bears no relation to the virus that causes distemper in dogs. The disease is destructive, highly contagious, and often fatal. Fortunately, it is less common than it once was, thanks, no doubt, to effective vaccines. Without early detection and treatment, the infected cat becomes desperately ill. Onset occurs four to six days after exposure, and early signs may include appetite loss, depression, fever, and vomiting yellow bile. Because the virus often attacks the lining of the small intestine, a sick cat may have a painful abdomen and may cry out pitifully if touched in that area. Typically, an infected cat crouches in a stiff, hunched-up manner over its water bowl, as if wanting to drink but unable to. A lowered white blood cell count (leukopenia) confirms the diagnosis and gives the disease its name.

Feline Leukemia Virus (FeLV)

First discovered in 1964, FeLV is a retrovirus that suppresses the bone marrow and the immune system, rendering the feline vulnerable to various cancers, such as leukemia, and other secondary ailments. Symptoms vary but generally include weight loss, anemia, poor appetite, lethargy, and recurring infections. An infected cat may seem healthy for years before succumbing to a FeLV-related illness, but testing is available to determine FeLV status. The first FeLV vaccine took about 20 years to develop. Immunity is initiated with two injections spaced about a month apart, followed by annual boosters. Recent research has raised concerns about a low incidence of tumors (fibrosarcomas) developing at the injection sites of FeLV (and rabies) vaccines. While not caused by the vaccines directly, the tumors appear to result from a profound localized inflammation some cats experience, perhaps in reaction to aluminum compounds used in the vaccine suspension. As the matter remains under investigation, not all veterinarians recommend FeLV vaccination for *all* cats. Some recommend it only for cats at risk of contracting the disease, so be sure to discuss this issue with your veterinarian so you can make an informed choice. FeLV is the leading infectious cause of death in cats, and if your exotic gets it, there is no cure. Keep in mind that tumor development is extremely rare, as few as a dozen cases for every 100,000 FeLV (or rabies) vaccines given. Unvaccinated cats face a far greater risk of developing fatal disease if exposed to the virus.

Cats allowed outdoors have the highest risk of FeLV exposure and certainly should be vaccinated. Others at risk include those living in multicat households and those exposed to outdoor cats, whether through direct contact or through screened windows. To be safe, any cat that comes into contact with other cats through breeding programs, at boarding kennels, or at cat shows needs protection against FeLV. Breeding toms and queens should be tested and certified free of the virus. Ideally, kittens should be tested before vaccination to rule out disease, because they can acquire the virus from an infected mother through the placenta or through the breast milk. If FeLV-positive, vaccination will neither help nor harm them. Because the disease passes from cat to cat through bite wounds and prolonged casual contact, all FeLV-positive cats should be kept indoors and isolated from FeLV-negative cats, even vaccinated ones. There is no evidence that FeLV is capable of causing disease in people.

Rabies

One of few feline ailments transmissible to humans, rabies occurs in nearly all warm-blooded animals. Skunks, foxes, raccoons, cats, and dogs account for most sporadic outbreaks. The fatal virus passes from an infected animal's saliva through a bite, open wound, or scrape. People bitten by a rabid animal must undergo a series of injections in order to save their lives.

Once inside the body, the virus travels to the brain, where it produces two characteristic forms: furious and paralytic, or "dumb," rabies. In the furious phase, cats exhibit personality changes that progress from subtle to severe. Normally affectionate and sociable cats may withdraw and hide. Aloof cats may become more loving, but in a few days, most infected animals become irritable and dangerously aggressive. Animals in this "mad dog" stage often act frenzied and deranged and will attack viciously without provocation. In the dumb phase, paralysis overtakes the body, starting with the face, jaw, and throat muscles. Unable to swallow its own saliva, the afflicted feline drools or "foams at the mouth." Eventually, the rear legs give way, and the cat can no longer stand or walk. Death soon follows.

Fortunately, regular vaccination easily prevents this merciless disease. Because of the threat to human health, most localities have laws requiring immunization of dogs and cats. To guarantee a certain immunity level, an initial rabies vaccine requires a booster one year later. Thereafter, some regions permit boosters that last for three years. Without question, all outdoor cats should be immunized against rabies because of their potential exposure to infected animals, wild or domestic. Even if your exotic stays indoors, keep its rabies immunization current in case it bites someone or gets outdoors accidentally. If your cat bites someone, you will need legal proof of current immunization from your veterinarian.

Feline Infectious Peritonitis (FIP)

This potentially fatal illness is caused by a coronavirus that spurs an inflammatory reaction in the blood vessels and body tissues. The disease strikes primarily younger and older cats and those debilitated by other illnesses, such as feline leukemia virus. Common signs include fever, lethargy, appetite and weight loss, and an overall unthrifty appearance. FIP typically takes one of two forms, wet or dry. The wet form involves fluid buildup in the abdomen and chest. An afflicted cat exhibits labored breathing, extreme depression, and a swollen belly. The dry form progresses more slowly and affects many organs, including the liver, kidneys, pancreas, brain, and eyes. Because symptoms are often vague, the dry form is more difficult to diagnose. The first FIP vaccine became available in 1991 and is given through nose drops. Most veterinarians recommend it only

If your exotic suddenly abandons its litter box training and begins soiling the house, it may have a lower urinary tract disorder. Signs include visiting the litter box frequently, urinating in unusual or inappropriate places, straining to urinate, and passing blood in the urine. Consult a veterinarian.

if the exposure threat is high. The disease poses a greater hazard in catteries and multicat households, so discuss this vaccine option with your veterinarian.

Feline Immunodeficiency Virus (FIV)

Discovered in 1987, FIV is a retrovirus in the same family as FeLV and human immunodeficiency virus (HIV), the virus that causes AIDS. Although FIV is sometimes called "feline AIDS," it is important to understand that people cannot catch this disease from cats. FIV is a species-specific virus, meaning that it infects only cats and is not transmissible to humans or to other animal species. The disease appears to be transmitted among cats mainly through bites. Because they often engage in territorial fighting, free-roaming males have the highest risk of contracting FIV. Cats kept indoors have the least risk. A test confirms a cat's FIV status, although no cure and no approved vaccines currently exist. Once contracted, the disease persists for life, although a cat may remain

healthy for months or years before its immune system weakens enough to allow secondary infections to take hold. Symptoms vary but usually include lethargy, weight loss, gum disease, and chronic infections. The best prevention to date simply involves avoiding contact with potentially infected cats, which means keeping your exotic indoors. Also, it's a good idea to have all new cats coming into your household tested for FIV (and FeLV) before exposing them to your exotic.

Feline Lower Urinary Tract Disease (FLUTD)

The urinary tract collects and disposes of urine through the bladder and a tube called the urethra. In female cats, the urethra is short and wide, whereas, in males, this opening through which urine passes is longer and more narrow. For this reason, males are more prone to urinary tract blockages than females, although problems can occur in both sexes. In FLUTD, often called FUS for feline urologic syndrome, tiny mineral crystals form in the lower urinary tract and irritate the internal tissues. In response to this discomfort, the cat may repeatedly lick its penis or vulva and urinate in unusual places, such as the bathtub. Feeling an uncomfortable urgency to urinate, the cat may make frequent trips to the litter box. The cat even may strain or cry as it attempts to void. Some people mistake this straining to urinate for constipation. If you notice these symptoms, or if you see blood in the urine, take your cat to a veterinarian immediately. If the crystals are large enough, they may block the urethra completely, creating a life-threatening emergency. If the cat cannot eliminate its urine, the kidneys may sustain irreversible damage from the backup pressure. Within a short time, toxic wastes can build up in the blood with fatal consequences. With prompt medical treatment, most cats recover; however, recurrences are common. Often, bacterial infections in the bladder or urethra complicate matters. The veterinarian may prescribe medications and dietary changes to manage the condition.

Parasites

Internal parasites: The most common internal parasites that plague cats include roundworms, hookworms, and tapeworms. Heartworms, common in dogs, rarely infest cats, except in some humid regions, where the mosquito, the host organism, strongly prevails. In such high-risk areas, preventive prescription drugs may be warranted. Ask your veterinarian.

An infected queen can pass certain worms to her kittens through the placenta and through the breast milk. So, during your exotic's first visit to the veterinarian, request a stool analysis, which unveils the presence of most worms. Because deworming drugs can cause toxic reactions, they should be administered only under veterinary supervision. Parasite prevention includes keeping cats indoors, maintaining good sanitation, and controlling fleas, lice, cockroaches, mosquitoes, and other vermin.

Kittens get roundworms from their infected mothers or through contact with contaminated cat feces. Signs include vomiting, diarrhea, weight loss, a potbellied appearance, and overall poor condition. Roundworms passed in vomit or stool look like white, wriggling spaghetti strands.

Hookworms, more prevalent in hot, humid areas, are picked up from soil infested with the larvae. Symptoms include anemia, diarrhea, weight loss, and black, tarry stools. Lungworms, acquired from contact with infected cats or from eating infected birds and rodents, migrate to a cat's lungs and

Fleas can carry tapeworm larvae, which your exotic ingests as it grooms itself. After the larvae grow in long, segmented strands in the cat's intestines, some break off and are eliminated in the feces. Some of these segments, which look like grains of rice, may cling to the hair around the cat's anus.

cause a dry, persistent cough. Flukes, although uncommon, can be ingested by eating infected raw fish and other small prey. Cats allowed outdoors should be checked for worms during their annual physical checkups.

Tapeworms, the most common internal parasites found in adult cats, are transmitted by rodents and fleas. During grooming, cats ingest fleas, which often carry immature tapeworms. The tapeworm larvae mature inside the cat's intestines, feeding on nutrients within and growing into long, segmented strands. When passed in the stool, fresh tapeworm segments look like grains of white rice. Some segments may stick to the hair around the anus, and when dry, they look like tiny seeds. Left untreated, tapeworms can rob the cat of important nutrients,

Cream and white exotic shorthair.

damage a cat's coat and skin from excessive scratching.

Even indoor cats can attract fleas from the outside. Following a whiff of a warm-blooded animal, the tiny insects can jump through holes in window screens or ride in on a person's clothing or shoes in search of a suitable host. Once indoors, fleas lay eggs on the host and turn your cat's plush fur into a virtual nursery for hundreds more. As the cat moves and scratches, the eggs fall off into carpets, upholstery, and bedding, where they hatch into larvae. The larvae feed on debris among deep carpet fibers, an indoor environment that mimics their natural habitat—grass. Frequent vacuuming helps control this stage, but throw out the bag afterward.

Flea control efforts fail if you concentrate only on killing the adult insects. Because fleas develop through four complex life stages—eggs, larvae, pupae, adults—your arsenal must include sprays, powders, or foggers targeted to kill fleas at various life cycles. Flea foggers, for example, treat entire rooms with a penetrating blast of insecticide, but if you select one that kills only adults, you miss the immature stages ready to hatch soon in your carpets. Shop for foggers that contain an insect growth regulator (IGR), a chemical that stops the eggs and larvae from fully developing and offers some residual effect. Because most compounds do not penetrate the hard-shell pupal stage, repeat all indoor treatments in two weeks to kill the emerging adults. Severe infestations may require a professional exterminator's services. Used as directed, IGRs are considered safe, and many on-pet products now contain these compounds for better flea control.

Before activating flea foggers, remove cats, fish, birds, and other animals from the environment. Cover or remove foodstuffs, as well as food and water dishes, so they will not be conta-

but rarely cause any outward clinical signs. For effective treatment, combine deworming agents with appropriate flea control measures.

External parasites—fleas: Fleas are the most common external parasites to plague cats and frustrate their owners. Easy to spot, fleas leave behind evidence of their visits to the host in the form of "flea dirt," which looks like fine grains of black sand in the cat's fur. To inspect for flea dirt, rub your hand against your cat's fur along its back and near the neck and tail and look closely at the skin for tiny black specks. Because fleas feed on your cat's blood, the pepper-like granules are really flea excrement from digested blood. If dampened, the tiny specks dissolve into bloody smudges. Left untreated, flea infestations can cause anemia from blood loss and minated by the insecticidal spray. Thoroughly air out the room(s), according to the label directions, before allowing animals (and humans) to reenter the treated area.

If you are uncomfortable with the idea of using pesticides in your home or on your pet, *sodium polyborate* products offer a less toxic alternative. Marketed through pet retail and mail-order firms, this white, crystalline powder is applied to carpeted areas and beat well into the pile. The compound acts as a stomach poison on flea larvae feeding among treated carpet fibers, hampering further lifestage development. Sodium polyborate has only a limited effect on adult fleas through desiccation, causing some to dry out or die of dehydration. For this reason, the "clearing out" process with this product is slow, taking from two to five weeks to eliminate an infestation. One application to dry carpet lasts about a year; however, being water-soluble, sodium polyborate is useless for outdoor flea control, and likewise, dissolves to ineffectiveness when you shampoo the carpets.

Note: Sodium polyborate is sometimes confused with ordinary borax or boric acid, which should *not* be used for flea control because of their potential toxicity to cats.

In addition to treating carpets and upholstered furniture, flea control involves bathing the cat, washing or replacing pet bedding, and spraying the lawn. An endless array of sprays, dips, powders, shampoos, and flea collars clutters the market. So, when choosing one chemical to use on your exotic and another to treat its environment, be careful to avoid potentially toxic combinations. Ask your veterinarian to recommend appropriate flea control products that can be used together safely.

Also, select only products labeled as safe for cats and follow the directions carefully. *Never use products*

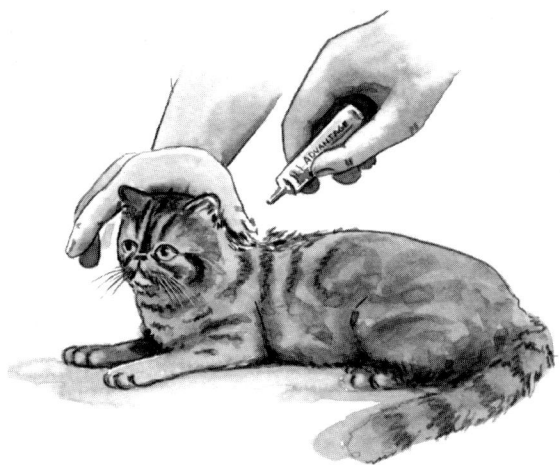

Advantage, a new once-a-month, topical flea control product, is easily and conveniently applied by parting the hair at the base of the neck, near the shoulder blades, and dabbing the tube contents directly onto the skin. It is available through veterinarians by prescription.

meant only for dogs. Select flea collars that have elastic or breakaway sections to prevent strangling, in case the cat gets caught on an object. Let flea collars air out a day or two before fastening them on your cat. Never use any product on a kitten or debilitated cat without veterinary approval.

For outdoor flea control, various sprays are available in lawn and garden shops. If you dislike the idea of spraying pesticides on your lawn, consider the environmentally friendly flea-eating nematodes available at feed stores and pet shops. When sprayed on your yard, these microscopic "bugs" gobble up flea larvae and reportedly do not harm beneficial insects, children, or animals. One application lasts about six weeks.

Some new once-a-month flea control products promise greater convenience and effectiveness in the war on fleas. A new topical product, Advantage (imidacloprid), is dabbed on the back of the cat's neck once a month. The active ingredient spreads across the entire animal and kills adult fleas before they can lay eggs and before they bite and irritate the cat. The product kills fleas by impairing their nervous system. Because its effectiveness appears to diminish if the cat's fur gets wet, it is not usually recommended for outdoor cats routinely exposed to wet weather elements.

The product PROGRAM (lufenuron) is mixed in the cat's food and taken internally. Fleas must bite and drink the host's blood for the drug to work. In this manner, the drug causes female fleas living on the host to produce infertile eggs. Male fleas are unaffected. Although useful for controlling indoor flea infestations, the drug obviously is not a cure-all for cats that suffer allergic reactions to flea bites. Both Advantage and PROGRAM are available by prescription through veterinarians.

Other external parasites: Besides fleas, cats sometimes play host to ticks, lice, and mites. Ticks burrow their heads into the skin and suck blood. Remove them promptly by grasping the body as close to the skin as possible with tweezers. Pull the tick straight out (without twisting) with firm, gentle traction. Because some ticks carry Lyme disease, which humans can catch, take precautions to control them if you choose to allow your exotic outdoors. Ask your veterinarian to recommend a suitable insecticide. Some flea-control products also help repel ticks.

Uncommon in well-kept, healthy cats, lice look like white specks (nits) stuck to the fur. Clipping the coat and bathing with a medicated shampoo gets rid of them. Mites, being microscopic, are harder to see, but signs of their presence include itchiness, hair loss, crusty sores, scaly dandruff, and body odor. Before prescribing appropriate treatment, a veterinarian needs to identify the specific mite variety through examination.

Ear mites: The most common mite found on cats is the ear mite, which lives in the ear canal and produces a crumbly, dark brown, foul-smelling, waxy discharge. While healthy ears are clean and pink inside, a waxy, brown buildup in the ears may indicate ear mites. An infected cat also may shake its head and scratch its ears. Prompt treatment prevents spread to the inner ear, where an infection can lead to deafness. Staggering and loss of balance may indicate inner ear problems that need immediate medical attention. Because ear mites are contagious, other cats and dogs in the household may require treatment as well.

Skin Problems

Ringworm: This itchy disorder is not caused by a worm at all, but rather by a fungus. Signs include scaly skin and patchy hair loss. Because people can catch this skin infection from cats, prompt veterinary treatment and disinfection of pet bedding are essential. Treatment may include clipping the coat, bathing the skin, and administering topical or oral medications. A new vaccine is available, so discuss this option with your veterinarian.

Flea allergy dermatitis: Some cats are so allergic to flea saliva, that the bite from a single flea will send them into a frenzy, scratching, biting, and licking to get at the culprit. The severe itching lasts long after the flea leaves, so you may never even see a parasite on the pet. Such sensitivity can lead to an uncomfortable and unsightly skin condition called flea allergy dermatitis. Besides itchiness, other symptoms include hair loss, patchy redness (called "hot spots"), and scabby, crusty sores on the skin. In addition to prescribed medications, aggressive and diligent flea control measures lessen the condition's severity and occurrence.

Common Allergies

Like people, cats can be allergic to a host of things in their environment, including pollen, weeds, grasses, mold spores, house dust, feathers, wool, insect stings, drugs, chemicals, and food ingredients. But instead of sneezing, watery eyes, and runny noses, cats' symptoms more likely involve itchy skin, face, and ears. Typical warning signs include rubbing against furniture or carpet and excessive scratching, licking, or chewing at itchy places. Gastrointestinal symptoms like vomiting and diarrhea also can occur, particularly if the allergen, or allergy-causing substance, is ingested in a food or drug. Redness, crusty skin and hair loss around the nose, mouth and face suggests a food allergy, or even an allergy to plastic feeding dishes. In the latter case, replacing plastic dishes with ceramic or stainless steel ones may offer an easy remedy.

Unfortunately, most allergy cases are not so simple. Testing exists, but allergies remain difficult to diagnose. Treatment varies widely from patient to patient, depending on the cause and symptoms, and may include antihistamines or allergy shots. Recovery can take a long time and because allergies usually persist for a lifetime, owners must commit to avoiding or reducing the allergen in the cat's environment for as long as the animal lives.

Tooth and Gum Care

Healthy gums are pink; diseased gums are tender, red, and swollen. Dental disease allows bacteria to leak into the bloodstream from sore, infected gums, compromising your cat's immune system and overall health. Plaque and tartar buildup on the teeth cause gingivitis. Left untreated, the gums begin to recede

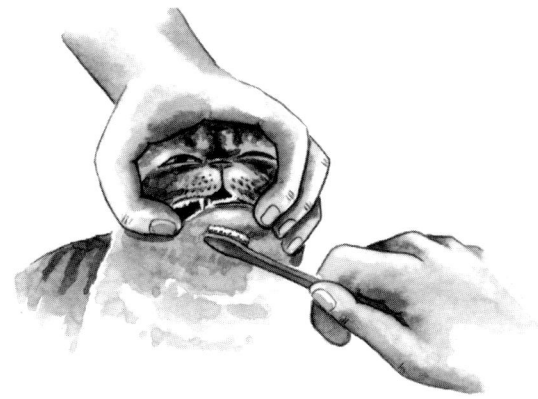

To brush your cat's teeth, grasp the head from above with one hand, using the fingers to hold open the corners of the lips. With the other hand, gently brush the teeth with a soft toothbrush or your finger wrapped in gauze. Cleaning the inside of the teeth is usually not necessary.

gradually and the teeth loosen. Besides bad breath, a cat with dental problems may have difficulty eating because its teeth and gums hurt. As a result, it may lose weight and condition. A cat with sensitive teeth also may flinch when you try to stroke the side of its face. The best way to prevent such discomfort is to regularly brush or rinse your cat's teeth with oral hygiene products designed for use in animals. Exotics tend to require more dental care than some other breeds. So, from time to time, you may need to have your cat's teeth professionally cleaned. For this procedure, the cat is anesthetized, and the veterinarian uses an ultrasonic scaler to blast away the ugly, brown tartar and polish the teeth.

Brushing Your Cat's Teeth

To get your exotic accustomed to having its mouth gently opened and handled, start early, while it's still a kitten. An older cat takes more time to

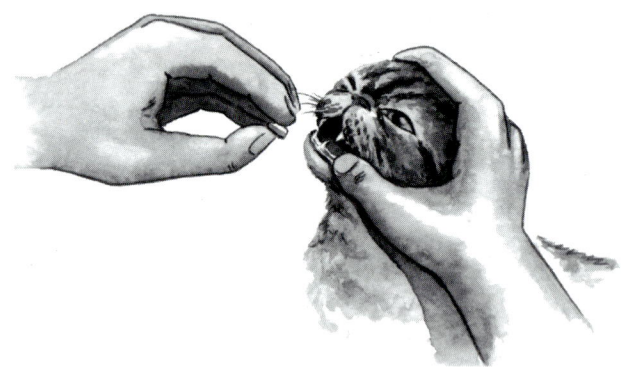

To give your exotic a pill, grasp the head with your thumb and index finger on the cat's cheekbones, then tilt back the head. Gently pry open the jaws and drop the pill into the back of the throat. Hold the cat's mouth shut and stroke its throat to encourage swallowing.

train and may never be completely cooperative.

Purchase a small pet toothbrush with ultra-soft bristles or one designed to fit over your finger tip for easier use. Also, select a non-foaming, enzymatic toothpaste made especially for animals.

Brown tabby exotic shorthair.

These pastes, designed to dissolve plaque without a lot of scrubbing action, come in fish, poultry, and malt flavors for finicky felines. *Never* use human toothpaste on a cat because it burns the back of the throat and, if swallowed, can cause stomach upset.

To begin training, dip your finger in something tasty, such as canned cat food juice, and gently rub the cat's teeth and gums. After about a week of doing this, try using the brush on only a few teeth on one side of the mouth. If your cat doesn't accept the brush right away, wrap gauze around your finger and gently massage the teeth and gums. With each try, clean a few more teeth, until your cat gradually accepts the process without a fuss. If the cat struggles, don't force it to submit. Instead, be extra gentle and patient, so it won't learn to dread having its mouth handled. Offer lots of praise and a tasty treat afterward.

Medicating Your Exotic

Getting your exotic used to having its mouth opened and handled will make it much easier for you to give it pills, should the need arise. Otherwise, the ordeal is likely to be a two-person job. If necessary, restrain the cat by wrapping its body in a towel with only the head sticking out. To medicate your cat, grasp the head with your thumb and index finger on its cheekbones and tilt back the head. Pry open the jaws with your finger, drop the pill into the back of the throat, then hold the cat's mouth shut and stroke its throat until it swallows. To administer liquid medication, tilt the head back, insert an eyedropper into the corner of the mouth and gently squirt in a few drops at a time. Do not squirt the medication into the cat's mouth too quickly or too forcefully, because the cat may accidentally inhale the liquid, which could lead to pneumonia. Hold the cat's mouth shut until it swallows.

Red tabby exotic shorthair.

Some medications can be mixed in the cat's food, if they are not too bitter tasting. Cats can easily detect medications added to their food and usually eat around the edges or refuse the food altogether. Sometimes, lacing the drug with tuna oil or concealing it in strong-smelling, fish-flavored canned food works but more often, administering the pill or liquid directly by mouth is the answer. When adding medication to food, make sure your other animals do not consume it.

If your cat's condition calls for injections, eye ointments, ear drops, or force-feeding that you must do at home, ask your veterinarian to demonstrate the best method of application. Make sure you understand how and when to administer any medication before you attempt to do it yourself, and know what to expect in terms of recovery time and side effects.

Never give your exotic any over-the-counter painkillers meant for humans, such as aspirin or Tylenol, which contains an ingredient called *acetaminophen* that is especially deadly to cats.

Preventing Hair Balls

Cats swallow a lot of hair when they groom themselves. This swallowed hair accumulates in the stomach and normally creates no problem. The hair mass simply moves through the digestive tract and gets eliminated in the usual way. Occasionally, however, a hair mass gets too large and may cause a blockage, requiring an enema or even surgery to remove. Signs of a blockage include frequent vomiting and refusal to eat.

Occasionally, cats spit up tubular masses of ingested hair, called hair balls. Before the cat vomits a hair ball, it will crouch and cough a few times in a dry, hacking, wheezing manner. Except for the mess, vomiting a hair ball is no cause for concern, unless it becomes too frequent, in which case you need to offer some remedy.

To prevent hair balls, groom your exotic regularly. Brushing and combing removes the dead hair it would swallow otherwise. If your cat displays the typical "hair ball cough," administer one of various petrolatum-based hair ball remedies recommended by your veterinarian. Or dab some plain petroleum jelly on your cat's paw for it to lick off. These products help lubricate the hair mass so that it expels more easily. Grass also seems to act as a purgative to help cats expel excess hair from the stomach. You can grow a fresh supply of grass indoors for your cat, and some pet stores sell grass kits for this purpose. Providing some greenery for your cat to nibble on also may help keep it away from your house plants.

Vital Signs

Taking a cat's temperature is a procedure few of them relish or submit to readily. While this chore is best left to your veterinarian, sometimes it may be necessary for you to do it yourself. To take a cat's temperature, use a rectal thermometer designed for human infants. Shake the mercury down to well below 100°F (38°C). Lubricate the thermometer with petroleum jelly and, while restraining the cat, insert with a gentle twisting motion into the anus about an inch. Hold in place for two minutes. Wipe clean to read. Normal body temperature ranges from 100 to 102.5°F (37.8–39°C), with the average being about 101.5°F (38.6°C). Any higher than 102.5°F (39.2°C) is cause for concern. To take a cat's pulse, feel for it high up on the inside hind leg. Normal pulse rate ranges from 100 to 180 beats per minute. Normal respiration is 20 to 30 breaths per minute. Ask your veterinarian to show you how to take these vital signs.

Euthanasia and Pet Loss

Unfortunately, the sad side of pet ownership is that cats have a shorter lifespan than people and eventually, owners have to let go and say goodbye. Although difficult and painful, the decision to euthanize a cat is sometimes the last and kindest gift we can offer a long-time companion suffering or debilitated from illness, injury, or old age. An anesthetic overdose administered by a veterinarian simply "puts the cat to sleep" without pain. Some veterinarians allow owners who request it to remain with the cat during the brief procedure, and many help handle cremation or burial arrangements.

For many people, losing a cherished cat companion causes as much trauma and heartbreak as losing a human loved one. This is not surprising, since the grieving process is essentially the same, and often, our pets have shared our daily lives more closely than our relatives or human friends. However, some people simply don't understand how much it hurts to lose an animal friend. These unenlightened folks may make well-meaning but misguided comments, such as, "It was only a cat! Just get another one!" that belittle the special bond you had with your cat. Don't listen to them. Instead, talk to people who understand your grief. Find out if your area has pet grief counseling and support groups to help people through this crisis. Ask your veterinarian for details.

Giving another cat a good home is a beautiful way to honor your deceased friend's memory. Some people want to get another cat right away, while others feel a need to let some time pass. Another cat will not replace the one you lost, but when you feel ready, you can build a new relationship with another cat that will be as uniquely special and joyful.

Understanding Exotic Behavior

Exotic Body Language

Exotics can communicate eloquently with their feline and human companions. As the owner, you need to know how to interpret your cat's body language so you can judge its moods. When your exotic is happy to see you, it approaches with ears pricked forward and tail held high. At sight of a stranger, a timid or submissive cat crouches, lowers its ears and drops its tail. A frightened or defensive cat makes itself appear as big as possible by arching its back and bristling its fur to full fluff. An angry cat crouches low, as if poised to attack. It flicks its tail from side to side, flattens its ears and sometimes hisses loudly or utters a low, drawn-out growl as a warning.

Often, cats that know each other well will play and move through these stances in a seemingly ferocious manner. Their playful encounters usually culminate in a gleeful chase through the house. These mock fights help them stay fit and keep their skills honed for the real thing. In a real confrontation, two cats may remain tense and still for several minutes, usually until one makes a strategic withdrawal. Being sensible creatures, cats generally observe territorial good manners and avoid unnecessary fighting.

Vocal Language

Although cats have an extensive vocal repertoire, they seldom speak unless you fail to get the message otherwise. They will lead you to their empty food bowl, and when no food is forthcoming, they will resort to plaintive mews. Generally, the more urgent the request, the louder the meow. A loud, throaty howl can mean your cat feels distressed—maybe it's gotten accidentally shut in a closet. Females in heat belt out a particularly annoying yowl, and mother cats chirp softly when calling their kittens. According to the intonation, a cat's meow can express many moods and needs. In time, your exotic will train you to understand its personal vocabulary of sounds and

A friendly cat that is pleased and happy to see you approaches with ears pricked forward and tail held high.

59

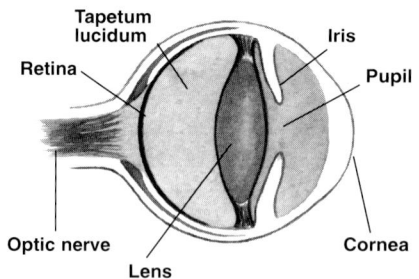

Tapetum lucidum — Iris — Retina — Pupil — Optic nerve — Lens — Cornea

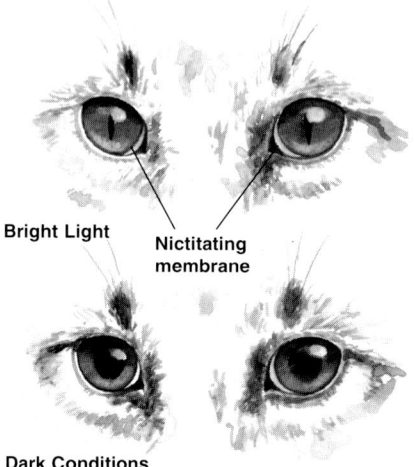

Bright Light

Nictitating membrane

Dark Conditions

A cat's eyes appear to glow in the dark because a special layer of cells in the eye, called the tapetum lucidum, *acts like a mirror, reflecting available light back onto the retina. This gives the cat its exceptional night vision.*

body postures. Soon, you will find yourself talking back and swearing that your exotic understands every word you say. Sharing this secret language is an important part of the bonding process between cats and humans, and ideally, you will come to feel that no one else can understand or care for your cat as well as you do.

Purring

Undoubtedly, the most universally recognized and beloved feline sound is the purr, thought to be produced by vibrations in the vocal cords as the cat breathes in and out. One of many simple pleasures of cat ownership, relaxing with a purring cat in your lap relieves stress, promotes a mutual sense of well-being, and strengthens the human/feline bond. Cats purr when they feel happy, secure, warm, and well-fed. But they also have been known to purr when they're hungry, hurt, upset, sick, and even dying. It is believed that cats purr not only to express pleasure and contentment, but also, under adverse circumstances, to calm and comfort themselves.

Your Exotic's Senses

Much of the mystery associated with cats results from the unique anatomy of their five senses, which are far superior to ours. Understanding how your exotic perceives its world helps explain many behaviors that seem incomprehensible otherwise.

Sight

Cats possess poor color vision, but they see well in dim light. Uniquely suited to hunting and stalking, their eyes are especially adept at detecting slight movements made by prey animals. A stalking cat will crouch patiently for long periods, staring at seemingly nothing, until its camouflaged prey finally reveals its whereabouts with barely a twitch. A special layer of cells behind the retina, called the *tapetum lucidum,* makes a cat's eyes appear to glow in the dark. These cells act like a mirror, reflecting all available light back onto the retina and giving the cat its exceptional night vision.

The feline pupil can dilate much wider than the human eye, allowing the cat's eye to collect light more effectively in dim conditions. A cat that feels threatened, frightened, or defensive also dilates its pupils so it can see better over a wider area. On sunny days, a cat's pupils constrict to vertical slits to block out bright light.

Another special characteristic of the cat's eye is an opaque third eyelid, called the nictitating membrane, which helps protect and lubricate the eyeball. Although usually not visible under normal conditions, except occasionally when the cat is sleeping, the third eyelid protrudes from the eye's inside corner if the eye gets injured, irritated, or infected. The appearance of this film over the eyes also occurs with some diseases and warrants a veterinary examination if it persists beyond an occasional blink.

Smell

Cats possess an acute sense of smell. When two cats meet, they sniff each other about the head and anal area, where scent glands exude a myriad of personal information. Often, a cat greets a human friend in similar fashion, jumping in a person's lap to sniff the face, then turning to present its rear end for examination. Like many other mammals, cats have a special scent mechanism, called the vomeronasal or Jacobson's organ, in the roof of their mouths behind the incisor teeth that allows them to "taste" odor molecules. When using this organ, a cat curls its upper lip back and sniffs the air deeply with teeth bared and mouth partially agape. This odd-looking grimace is called the "flehmen response." Cats often display flehmen when examining urine and scent marks left by other animals. Researchers believe the special organ helps mammals find mates by sorting out sex-related scent hormones called pheromones.

Taste

Specialized cells on a cat's tongue enable it to detect the chemical components of food as they are dissolved in the mouth by saliva. These taste buds send signals to the brain along nerve pathways, where taste identification actually takes place. Taste tests suggest that cats can distinguish between salty or sour foods, but apparently they cannot taste simple sugars. Their preference, of course, is meat served at room temperature or near the body temperature of most small prey animals.

Touch

It's been said that if a cat's whiskers can pass through a small opening, the cat knows its body will fit through, too. While this may be more fancy than fact, it is true that whiskers are highly sensitive tactile organs. Cats use them to gauge the size of prey caught in their paws, to avoid objects in dim light, and to detect vibrations and changes in their environment. For these reasons, never clip your exotic's whiskers.

Hearing

Because its normal prey typically emits high-pitched sounds, a cat's ears are tuned to frequencies well beyond the range of human hearing. When a cat hears something, it swivels its ears toward the source and peers intently in the direction of the noise. Cats also learn to respond to certain words by recognizing the sounds of the first few letters, and your exotic will quickly learn its name if you consistently call to it in the same tone of voice at feeding time.

Balance and the Righting Reflex

If a cat rolls off a window sill and falls in an upside-down position, a balance mechanism in the inner ear enables it to rotate the forehand first, then the hindquarters, so that it automatically rights itself in mid-air and lands on all fours. Even with this remarkable reflex ability, however, cats that fall from great heights often sustain fractures and other injuries, recognized as high-rise syndrome, as discussed on page 25.

HOW-TO:
Dealing with Elimination Problems

Causes

Contrary to popular belief, cats do not eliminate outside of the litter box out of spite, but the behavior is often symptomatic of emotional anxiety or physical discomfort. Whenever a cat begins eliminating in inappropriate places, consider urinary tract infections and other medical causes first. Prompt veterinary treatment can reverse the problem before it becomes an established habit. Once disease is ruled out, pursue the behavioral approaches.

Solutions

Generally, when a housebroken cat eliminates outside its litter box, it is either marking territory or displaying a preference for a particular spot, surface, or litter material. Because the motivating factors usually are different, it's important to determine whether the cat is spraying vertical surfaces or squatting to urinate on horizontal surfaces. Sometimes the sight of outdoor cats or the introduction of a new pet or a new baby into the household can trigger territorial spraying. In this situation, veterinarians can prescribe drugs that may ease the cat's anxiety and help suppress spraying and aggressive behaviors.

A cat that squats on the carpet or floor may simply be expressing a dislike for the location of its litter box or for the

Before attempting to treat an elimination problem, it's important to determine whether the cat is squatting to urinate on horizontal surfaces, such as the floor, or spraying vertical surfaces to mark territory.

texture of the litter. Perhaps the box is near a noisy furnace that frightens the cat when operating. Try moving the box to a quieter area, or if possible, place it at or near the site of the "accident." For whatever reason, the cat may prefer that spot, and putting the box there may solve the problem.

If location doesn't seem to be a factor, experiment with different litter materials; some cats don't like litters treated with perfumes and deodorizers. Often, a problem arises because cat and owner have different opinions as to what constitutes a clean litter box. After all, digging in dirty, damp litter is like using an unflushed toilet. Be fastidious

about removing urine and feces daily and replacing soiled litter weekly, and your cat will be more happily inclined to continue using the box.

The number of cats in a household also can influence spraying and elimination behaviors. If you have more than one cat, provide each with its own litter box. Sometimes the more aggressive cat will chase another away from the litter box. If this happens, place the boxes far enough apart, even in separate rooms, to give each cat a sense of privacy and individual territory.

Whatever the cause, punishing a cat for spraying or eliminating in inappropriate places is seldom effective and often makes matters worse. Rubbing your cat's nose in the mess will only make it fear you. Spanking it, then carrying it to the litter box may backfire and actually cause it to associate the abuse and fear with the litter box.

Cleaning Up

To deter the cat from using the same location as a toilet again, clean up accidents with enzymatic products that dissolve the odor. Remember to clean the mat under the carpet, too, as the urine will have soaked through. Any traces of scent left will attract the cat back to the same spot. If you can't lift the carpet to clean under it, use a syringe to inject solution under the rug. Several good odor neutralizing products can be purchased at pet shops. Vinegar and water works fairly well, too. But avoid ammonia-based cleaners; ammonia is a urine byproduct and might attract the cat back to the spot.

After you thoroughly clean the spot, make the surface less appealing to the cat by covering

Sometimes, an aggressive cat will claim a litter box as its territory and chase others away. To prevent this, provide each cat in your household with its own litter box, and locate the boxes in separate rooms, if necessary.

it temporarily with plastic, aluminum foil, sandpaper, window screen, or double-sided sticky tape. If possible, keep the cat completely away from the area for awhile to break the habit. For further reinforcement, use a water pistol or make a loud noise to startle the cat away from the area every time you see it near the spot. For a different approach, try changing the significance of the area by placing food and water bowls there. Cats typically will not eliminate where they eat.

Multicat Households

Having more than one cat in the house can be rewarding to both cat and cat lover. The owner has an opportunity to compare and savor each feline's unique personality. The cats benefit by keeping each

After thoroughly cleaning an "accident" site, cover it temporarily with window screen, plastic sheeting, sandpaper, double-sided sticky tape, or some other covering that will make the surface unappealing to the cat. This will help deter the cat from using the same spot again.

other company while the owner is away at work all day. Despite their aloof, solitary reputation, cats clearly enjoy each other's companionship and are highly social animals. They generally adapt well to group living; however, confining too many cats in a limited space can increase the incidence of behavior problems. Signs of stress from overcrowding may include hiding, fighting, house-soiling, and excessive grooming.

Often, what people perceive as a behavior "problem" in the home is quite normal for cats in the wild. For instance, cats, being naturally territorial, mark and defend areas where they spend most of their time. Fortunately, when living in social groups, cats tend to claim less territory, and boundaries become more flexible. Individuals that bond as friends share space, sleep together, and groom each other. In general, the bigger your home, the fewer territorial problems your indoor cats are likely to develop. But if you have only so much room, expand the cats' available territory from floor to ceiling by installing vertical cat climbing trees and carpeted kitty condos. These carpet-covered cat trees with tiered sleeping shelves make excellent scratching posts and provide ample exercise and climbing opportunities for indoor cats.

Hunting Habits

As natural predators, cats are well-adapted with excellent vision for night hunting in near darkness. Typically, they catnap throughout the day and awake ready for action by evening. By bedtime, their hunting instincts rev into high gear, and your toes wriggling under the bed covers present the perfect prey to pounce upon. This nocturnal tendency probably contributed to the time-honored tradition of "putting the cat out" at night, no doubt so that a weary owner could get some sleep. Fortunately, indoor cats adapt readily to our diurnal timetables, and many sleep soundly all night on their owners' beds, doubling as fail-safe alarm clocks come morning. As with people, cats that get plenty of exercise generally sleep better.

To exercise your cat and watch its hunting instincts in action, play with it periodically, using an interactive toy, such as a kitty fishing pole with sparklers or feathers attached. Throw out the line and slowly reel in your exotic as it stalks the wriggling lure. Observe as your exotic crouches and creeps forward silently, pupils wide and eyes fixed, watching for the slightest move that might mean the "prey" is going to run. Muscles remain tensed and ready for instant pursuit. The tail twitches in anticipation. As the cat prepares to pounce, it wriggles its rear, treading quietly with the back legs, as if testing which foot will provide the better spring action. Before the feather flutters one last time, the cat springs upon it with claws extended, the front paws striking in deadly accuracy to pinion the prey. One well-placed bite with the powerful canine teeth ends the struggle.

Even people who despise predation confess to being entertained and awed by the cat's fluid body coordination and rigid concentration during play sessions. The ancient Egyptians worshipped the cat for its unequaled

Spaying or neutering your exotic eliminates or reduces the possibility of certain diseases occurring later in life that involve the male or female organs or that are influenced by the sex hormones.

When playing with a dangling lure attached to an elastic string, your exotic displays innate prey-catching behavior patterns, the same ones it would use when hunting prey in the wild.

rodent control talents, yet modern-day cat enthusiasts often experience a paradoxical twinge of guilt when their cat's natural instincts bring down a fledgling sparrow. Worse for some people are the times when their outdoor cat brings home prey as a gift offering and deposits the dead body on the doorstep. Experts say this normal behavior relates to the way cats perceive their human caretakers as family members. Mother cats instinctively bring dead or stunned prey to the nest when they teach their kittens how to recognize and hunt prey. So if your exotic delivers a similar offering to your "nest," don't punish the cat for behaving—well, like a cat. Simply praise your cat for its extraordinary generosity, then dispose of the "gift" quickly, so as not to prolong your exotic's exposure to potential parasites or disease harbored by the unfortunate prey. If predation disgusts you, you can prevent it by keeping your cat indoors. Your exotic certainly will remain safer and healthier without contact with diseased rodents or birds and other outdoor hazards, and it will be just as happy hunting and preying on store-bought catnip mice.

When your exotic rubs against you in greeting when you come home from a long day, it is not just trying to woo you into serving dinner early. It is marking you with scent from glands around its face, mouth, and tail.

Territorial Marking

Rubbing

Cats greet their owners by rubbing against their legs, but this endearing habit is more than an expression of affection—it is one means of territorial marking. By rubbing against furniture and other objects, cats leave behind scent from glands around their faces, mouths, and tails. Humans can't smell the scent, but other cats can. Because you're part of your cat's territory, your exotic really is saying, "You belong to me!" when it rubs against you and marks you with its scent. In addition, the mingling of your smell on the cat's fur helps identify you as part of its circle of friends.

Spraying

Less endearing is the feline habit of spraying urine to mark territory. Males are more prone to this behavior, but females sometimes do it to communicate their reproductive status, especially when in heat. Although spaying and neutering tend to curb this undesirable behavior, both sexes, whether whole or altered, may occasionally resort to spraying when engaged in a dispute with another cat over territory or dominance. This problem is more common in multicat households.

When a cat sprays, it stands, rather than squats, with its back to a vertical surface and its tail straight in the air. The tail quivers as the cat squirts urine to mark the wall, drapery, or furniture leg.

Declawing involves surgical amputation of the claw tips and the last bone of the toes.

Clawing

When a cat scratches the arm of the couch, it is not misbehaving. It is fulfilling an instinctive need to keep its basic defense weaponry—its claws—sharp and trim. Similar to filing fingernails, the in-and-out action on wood or rough fabric helps strip away the dead, outer layers of the claws. The action also marks the scratched object with scent from glands in the cat's paws. The scent, plus an apparent preference for the spot, draw the cat back to the same site to claw until the couch arm becomes a shredded mess. You cannot eliminate this natural clawing behavior, but you can modify it by providing the cat with an alternative scratching post and teaching your cat to use it. To avoid destructive clawing habits, begin training your kitten to use a scratching post as soon as you bring it home. (See page 23.)

Another alternative for dealing with clawing problems is to glue vinyl nail caps onto the cat's newly trimmed claws. The caps give the nails a soft, blunt tip and help prevent snags in carpets, furniture, and drapes. The major drawback to this method is that the vinyl caps have to be reapplied every four to six weeks, as the nails grow. The application is simple, however, and owners can purchase take-home kits and learn to manicure their cats' nails themselves. Ask your veterinarian to demonstrate the product. Vinyl nail caps are not recommended for outdoor animals because they inhibit a cat's ability to climb.

Declawing

Declawing is the least desirable alternative for dealing with destructive clawing and should be considered only as a last resort after other methods have failed. Banned in some countries, this controversial procedure involves putting the cat under anesthesia and surgically amputating the claw tip and the last bone of the toe. Generally, only the front claws are removed, because the hind feet are not used for scratching furniture. After the operation, the cat suffers some pain as its mutilated paws heal.

Declawing renders a cat ineligible for the show ring, because the major cat associations that sponsor shows disallow the practice. With only the front claws removed, a cat still can use its rear claws to climb trees. Yet, declawing inhibits a cat's ability to climb and defend itself against attackers to a degree. Cats allowed to roam outdoors have a clear disadvantage and, therefore, should not be declawed. Many people believe that robbing a cat of its natural defenses in this way harms it psychologically and may make it more apt to bite in self-defense. Some owners report profound personality changes in their cats after the surgery. Others say their cats developed inappropriate toilet habits afterward, probably as a result of litter irritating the tender incisions. Older cats seem to have more difficulty adjusting to life without claws than kittens.

Grooming Your Exotic

Sometimes called the "lazy man's Persian," exotic shorthairs do not require the daily grooming commitment that their longhaired relatives, the Persians and the Himalayans, demand. Nevertheless, the exotic's dense, plush coat is not entirely maintenance free. The exotic's undercoat grows extremely thick during winter, then sheds in spring and early summer. During the peak of shedding season, exotics require a good combing every other day or so to prevent matting. For the rest of the year, a weekly combing is sufficient to remove any loose, dead hair. Regular combing is a healthful practice because it helps prevent hair balls the inexpensive way. It also helps stimulate blood circulation in the skin and distribute natural oils through the coat, keeping it shiny and vibrant looking.

Fur serves to protect the cat from the elements. A cat's coat typically consists of a topcoat of "guard" hairs over a soft undercoat of "down" and "awn" hairs. The coarser guard hairs protect the dense underfur from the elements. The soft down hairs closest to the skin provide added warmth, while the awn hairs form a middle layer of insulation. The guard and awn hairs also can fluff out to trap air for better insulation.

Shedding

In addition to keeping the coat clean and mat-free, regular grooming minimizes the amount of cat hair left behind on your furniture and clothing. And yes, even shorthaired cats shed. While shedding is most noticeable in spring and fall, during the seasonal changes of hair coat, house cats living in artificial light shed a little bit year-round. Many people believe seasonal temperature changes cause cats to shed, but experts say environmental lighting governs this process. Under natural conditions, the lengthening sunlight hours in early spring trigger the cat's body to shed hair and grow a new coat in preparation for the changing season. Similarly, fall's shorter daylight hours cause the coat to thicken for winter. But when artificial lighting extends the daylight hours in the cat's environment year-round, this natural cycle seems to get confused.

You can easily make time for combing and brushing your cat while watching TV. Grooming keeps your exotic's coat clean, healthy, and mat-free, but it also provides an opportunity for a mutual and satisfying bonding between human and animal.

Blue exotic. Although exotics do not require the daily grooming Persians need, they still require regular combing and brushing to remove loose hairs from their plush, dense coat and to help keep the fur clean and shiny.

First Steps in Grooming

Most cats love the attention they get during grooming and learn to tolerate their beauty sessions readily. If you take time to accustom your exotic to the procedure early, starting at the kitten stage, and if you make each experience pleasurable, you will eventually be rewarded with a cat that looks forward to receiving your undivided attention during the sessions. To begin training your exotic kitten, spend a few minutes each day gently combing the fur with a small, fine-toothed metal comb. Keep the sessions short until the youngster gets used to being handled this way. Use the opportunity to get your exotic accustomed to having its mouth gently opened, its ears touched, and its paws handled. This extra effort will pay off later when brushing teeth, administering medications, cleaning ears, and trimming claws.

Don't restrain your exotic if its attention wanders elsewhere. Simply end the session and pick it up again later. While grooming, hold the animal in your lap, or place it on a counter or table. Establish a regular grooming location and routine, and your exotic will quickly learn what's expected of it when you take it to that spot and pick up the comb. Practice this routine daily for several weeks, then once your kitten accepts grooming graciously, gradually decrease the number of sessions to once or twice a week.

As your kitten grows, graduate to a medium size metal comb. For convenience and versatility, some combs come with closely spaced teeth on one end and wider-spaced teeth on the other end. Use the fine-toothed end on the shorter hair around the face, head, and chin. Use it also as a flea comb, handily trapping the parasites and their dirt in the closely spaced teeth. To dispatch the fleas, simply dip the comb in a nearby pan of water until the insects drown. Always end grooming sessions

The result is a coat that sheds slightly on a continual basis. In addition, overheated homes in winter may make some house cats prone to shed more than normal because their skin gets too dry.

If your exotic's skin ever looks dry or flaky, or if the coat appears dull, looks oily, smells bad, or feels brittle, schedule a visit to your veterinarian. Several medical and dietary problems can affect the skin and hair coat, including allergies, parasites, and hormonal or nutritional imbalances, among others. Also, as cats age, they need more grooming assistance from you, because their decreasing muscle and joint flexibility renders them less able to do as good a job of grooming themselves.

with a brief playtime, lots of praise, and maybe even a special treat, and your cat will eagerly anticipate the next one.

Combing and Brushing Methods

When combing, start at the base of the neck and gently comb the back and sides. Raise the chin a little to comb the throat and chest. When combing delicate areas, such as the belly, legs, and tail, be especially careful not to rake the comb's teeth against the cat's sensitive skin. To strip the coat during shedding season, brush the fur against the way the hair lies. This removes the loose, dead undercoat hairs trapped closer to the skin and helps prevent matting. To put the hair back in place, gently brush or comb through it a second time, going the way the hair lies.

Even if you have no plans to show your exotic, an occasional bath may be in order to clean the coat of flea dirt or excess oils. Intact males seem particularly prone to develop an oily condition called "stud tail," caused by overactive glands and characterized by a waxy brown buildup at the base and top ridge of the tail. If not periodically cleansed, the greasy accumulation can form a crust on the skin and infect the hair follicles, causing sores and hair loss on the tail. Neutering usually eliminates this tendency.

Removing Mats

Fortunately, the exotic's short coat renders it relatively mat-free most of the time. Except for an occasional mat in the "armpits" or on the belly, this particular grooming problem, more prevalent in longhaired breeds, seldom afflicts the shorthaired exotic. Longhaired exotics, like Persians, are quite prone to matting and require daily grooming to prevent this problem. Both varieties require more frequent combing during peak shedding season, when the undercoat sheds and mats more easily. It's important to

When bathing your exotic or when dipping and treating it for fleas, use only products that are labeled as safe for use on cats. Products designed for dogs may be too strong, even fatal, if used on cats.

remove any mat, no matter how small, right away. The longer a mat remains in the coat, the tighter it pulls the skin. If neglected too long, mats can irritate the skin severely enough to cause raw, open sores. Mats on the paw pads or between the toes can become especially painful and probably feel a lot like having a rock in your shoe.

Always remove any mats before bathing, too, because water will "set" them permanently and make removal much more difficult. To remove a mat, separate it with your fingers and work it loose without yanking on the skin. To gently pick a stubborn mat loose, use the end teeth of a wide-toothed comb. A dab of talcum powder, baby oil, or hair conditioner may help loosen a tight mat, but avoid using a greasy substance unless you're planning to bathe the cat afterward. Use scissors with care and as a last resort.

HOW-TO:
Bathing Your Exotic

If you are going to show your exotic, it will require a bath a day or two before the show. Otherwise, bathing a pet exotic shorthair becomes necessary only during a heavy flea season or if the coat gets oily or dirty. Remember, too many baths can rob the coat of natural oils and dry the skin, so bathe only when your cat truly needs it.

Assemble all of your supplies before you start bathing your exotic. You will need cat-safe shampoo, a comb, cotton balls, several towels, a wash cloth, a sink or two tubs (one for washing, one for rinsing), a pitcher or shower spray attachment, and a blow dryer.

Things You'll Need

Every breeder and exhibitor has special preferences when it comes to shampoos and such, so start with what your breeder recommends. Use only products labeled safe for cats. *Never* use dog shampoos or dog flea products on a cat, because the medication or flea insecticide in canine preparations may be too strong, even fatal, for cats. Also, not all cat flea products are safe for use on kittens, so read labels carefully before applying any shampoo, spray, dip, or powder to a kitten's fur. If the label doesn't specifically say that the product is safe for use on kittens, don't risk using it. Start getting your kitten used to baths after age four months, but don't overdo it.

In addition to shampoo, other supplies you'll need for the bath include:
• a comb
• cotton balls (for swabbing the ears)
• a blow dryer
• towels
• a wash cloth
• a sink or tub
• a pitcher or shower spray attachment
• a source of clean, warm water for washing and rinsing.

The kitchen sink is usually the ideal place for the job, but if you must bathe the cat in a laundry tub, reserve a second tub of clean water for rinsing. For blow drying the cat, you'll need a table or countertop with access to an electrical outlet. You'll probably also need a willing assistant, because many cat baths easily turn into two-person productions, especially if the feline is not fond of or used to the idea.

Before You Start

To minimize the risk of injury to you and your assistant, trim the cat's claws first. Also before bathing, give the coat a thorough combing to remove mats or loose, dead hairs that could get tangled or set in wet fur.

If possible, close off the room where the bath will take place, so you won't have to

Spend twice as long rinsing as you do lathering. If using a spray nozzle, keep the water pressure low to avoid frightening the cat. Avoid spraying the cat in the face or getting soap near the eyes.

Towel dry first, then blow dry on a low heat setting to prevent the cat from chilling. Avoid blowing air in the cat's face.

chase a wet, soapy escapee through the house. Before putting the cat in the tub or sink, fill the basin partially with warm (not hot) water. A rubber bath mat in the bottom prevents slipping and makes the cat feel more secure by giving it something to grip.

How to Bathe

Have your assistant hold the cat down in the partially filled water basin with gentle pressure on the back and shoulders. If the cat panics, talk to it reassuringly and gently hold it down by the scruff of the neck until it stops struggling. Be careful not to splash water in the cat's face or dunk its head under, as this will only increase its panic and create havoc for you and your assistant.

Wet the fur first with warm water, using the pitcher to dip and pour over the cat's back. If using a spray nozzle, keep the water pressure low to avoid frightening the cat. Don't spray water directly in the face. After wetting the fur sufficiently, apply shampoo and form a lather, starting at the neck and working back toward the tail. To lather the belly, have your assistant hold up the front legs. Avoid getting soap near the face and eyes. Use a damp wash cloth or moistened cotton balls to gently wet the head and wipe the face and eye areas clean.

How to Rinse

To remove all traces of shampoo, spend twice as much time rinsing as you do lathering. Any residue left behind could make the coat look flat and greasy and cause itching and irritation. Use the spray nozzle to rinse, or put the cat in a tub of clean, warm water, then dip and pour the water from the pitcher. When the fur feels squeaky clean, drain off the water and gently press out the excess by running your hands down the back, legs, and tail.

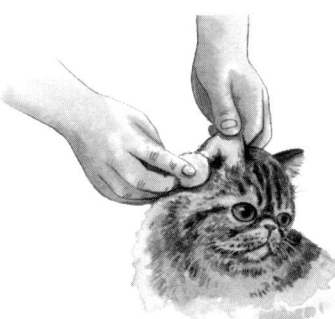

Gently wipe the inside of the ear flaps clean with cotton balls. If you use a cotton-tipped swab, be careful to never stick the end into the ear canal, as this could damage the cat's delicate hearing mechanisms.

Lift the cat out of the tub or sink, being careful to support its rear end with one hand, and place it on a table or counter-top for drying.

How to Blow Dry

After rinsing, completely dry your exotic with a blow dryer. First, towel dry the sopping fur as much as possible, but towel drying alone simply can't remove all of the moisture. Finishing with the blow dryer is necessary to prevent the cat from chilling. Like bathing, many cats learn to tolerate blow drying if you exercise some sensitivity when introducing them to the idea. Use only the low settings, never the hottest setting. And *never* blow air directly in the cat's face.

Gently comb the fur as you blow dry, or separate the damp hair with your fingers, starting at the neck and working back toward the tail. Don't forget to dry the underside. Have your assistant hold up the front legs for easier access to the belly and between the hind legs.

Cleaning the Ears

Finally, use cotton balls to gently wipe away any dirt or wax visible just inside the ear flaps. *Never* poke cotton swabs or other objects into the ear canal, as this could cause injury to the delicate inner ear structures. If the ears show an excessive amount of dirty, crumbly, brown wax inside, or if they exude a fruity odor, have your veterinarian check for ear mites or fungal infections.

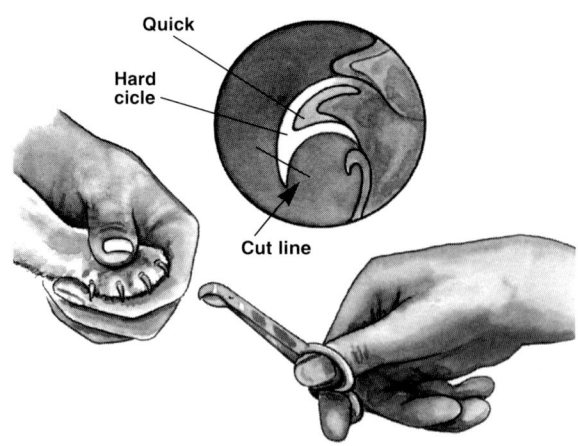

Quick

Hard cicle

Cut line

Claws need to be trimmed once a month or so. Clip only the white tips. Be careful not to cut into the pink "quick," as this will cause pain and bleeding.

Trimming Claws

In addition to bathing and brushing, toenail clipping is something you should get your exotic accustomed to at a young age. Like your fingernails, cats' claws grow continuously and need regular attention. Even with scratching posts available, an indoor cat's nails do not wear down as readily as an outdoor cat's. Neglected, untrimmed claws can curve under and grow back into the paw pads, causing a painful swelling and abscess. Trim claws once a month or so and always prior to a show. Regular trimming reduces the risk of injury to yourself and other pets and helps prevent snags in your carpets and furnishings.

Cats retract their claws when not in use. To extend them for trimming, hold the paw with your thumb on top and fingers on the bottom and gently squeeze. Before clipping, look closely at the nail and identify the "quick." If the nail is white, the quick clearly shows up as a thin pink line running about three-fourths of the way down the nail toward the tip. To avoid cutting into the sensitive quick, trim the nail tip below the pink line. The quick contains nerves and blood vessels, and if you accidentally cut into the pink, the cat will feel pain and the nail will bleed. If this happens, hold pressure over it with a cotton ball until the blood clots, or apply a shaving styptic.

With the cat held securely in your lap, trim the claws on the front and hind feet, starting with two or three nails at a time until your exotic gets accustomed to the idea. Use human or pet nail clippers for the job, then smooth the rough edges with an emery board or nail file. Don't forget the fifth claw slightly higher up on each inside forepaw.

Showing Your Exotic

Most people who own a purebred cat find themselves drawn to a cat show sooner or later, if for no other reason than to see how other cats of the same breed compare with their own. Besides being the best place to meet breeders and fellow feline lovers, cat shows are enjoyable and educational. You can learn a lot about cat care simply by observing the way exhibitors groom and ready their entries for the judging ring. Likewise, you can learn a lot about the different breeds by listening to judges' comments as they examine each cat. Large shows also attract numerous vendors that display and sell cat-motif gifts, toys, grooming aids, and accessories. Even if you never intend to show your exotic, attending a few cat shows will be rewarding adventures. To learn about upcoming shows in or near your area, check listings in cat fanciers' magazines. The cat-registering associations also can provide information about affiliated cat shows and clubs in your area.

How Cat Shows Began

History credits England with staging the prototype of today's cat competitions in 1871 at London's Crystal Palace. Harrison Weir organized the show and developed the first breed standards by which the cats were judged. He became president of that country's first cat club, the National Cat Club; which issued the first stud book in the late 1800s. Before long, numerous cat clubs sprang up in Great Britain, and the rivalry among them grew intense. By 1910, the Governing Council of the Cat Fancy (GCCF) was established with delegates from the various clubs to oversee the registering of pedigreed cats and to set the rules for all cat shows in Great Britain.

In the United States, cat exhibits and judgings have taken place since the 1870s, but an official all-breed

Neutered cats like this lovely cream and white van exotic can be shown in alter or "premiership" classes.

show held in 1895 at New York's Madison Square Garden marked the beginning of real interest among North American cat fanciers. In 1899, the first and oldest U.S. registry, the American Cat Association (ACA), was formed to keep records. Today, at least eight additional cat-registering associations exist in North America. They include the Cat Fanciers' Association (CFA), the American Cat Fanciers' Association (ACFA), The International Cat Association (TICA), the Cat Fanciers' Federation (CFF), the American Association of Cat Enthusiasts (AACE), the National Cat Fanciers' Association (NCFA), the United Feline Organization (UFO) and the Canadian Cat Association (CCA). Each association has its own show rules and breed standards, but all maintain stud books, verify pedigrees, charter clubs, register cats, sanction shows, and present awards. CFA, incorporated in 1919, is the world's largest registry of pedigreed cats, sponsoring approximately 400 shows a year across the United States and internationally through its more than 650 member clubs.

How a Cat Show Is Organized

In Great Britain, judges go from cage to cage examining cats; during some judging, they even ask owners to leave the show hall. In the United States, however, judging takes place on "judging tables" set up in one area of the show hall in full view of all spectators and exhibitors attending. Behind each judging table is a row of cages, where cats entered in the same category are called to await judging. This setup of tables and cages is called a *judging ring*. A single exhibition may have four or more judging rings set up, each operating as a separate competition and presided over by a different judge. Sometimes, separate clubs present back-to-back shows consisting of

eight to ten rings over a two-day weekend. Cats can compete in all rings for which they are eligible. In the ring, the judge removes each cat from its cage, places it on the judging table in view of the audience and thoroughly examines it. After evaluating all cats in the ring, the judge awards at least first-, second-, and third-place ribbons to the winners. All pedigreed cats are judged according to how closely they meet the written standard of perfection for their particular breed, pattern, and color.

The "All-Breed" Show

If the show is an "all-breed" show, all cats, regardless of their type, compete against each other. Specialty shows, on the other hand, may be restricted to longhaired or shorthaired breeds. Depending on the association sponsoring the show, various divisions and classes exist for eligible pedigreed cats, altered cats, kittens, household pets, and new or experimental breeds and colors. Generally, unaltered, adult pedigreed cats begin their show careers competing in "open" classes against others of their breed, sex, and color. After achieving a specified number of wins, they become a champion and can compete against other champions for the coveted title of grand champion. Many associations award additional titles beyond these.

Alter Classes

Alter classes, called "premiership" in the CFA, allow spayed and neutered pedigreed cats to compete against other altered cats of the same breed. Altered cats are judged according to the same standards as "whole" cats, but instead of qualifying as a champion or grand champion, they earn comparable titles of "premier" or "grand premier" in the CFA. Many novice exhibitors prefer to show in alter classes, because acquiring and owning a "show-alter" cat affords an opportunity to compete on equal footing with breeders who've been in the business for years. Yet, having a show alter relieves newcomers to the cat fancy of the extra commitment involved in keeping a breeding animal.

Kitten and Pet Classes

Pedigreed kittens between four and eight (or in some associations, ten) months of age can compete in classes with other kittens of their breed. The household pet (HHP) competition is for mixed-breed or non-pedigreed cats, which must be spayed or neutered. Policies vary, but some associations permit a purebred cat to be shown as a household pet, as long as the owner surrenders the papers or does not register the cat as a purebred. Household pets are judged for their beauty, personality, and overall condition, rather than against a formal breed standard.

New Breeds and Colors

Most shows allow experimental breeds and colors of cats to be exhibited in nonchampionship classes, which generally are called Provisional, Miscellaneous, or New Breeds and Colors (NBC). In CFA, for example, AOV (Any Other Variety) classes are designed for cats within a given breed that do not conform in some way, usually in color or coat length, to their current breed standard, and therefore, are not yet allowed in championship competition. Longhaired exotics, for example, are currently eligible only for showing as AOVs in CFA. As such, they cannot compete for titles or Best in Show.

Practices for accepting and showing new breeds, colors, and varieties differ among the associations. In general, experimental breeds are exhibited first in noncompetitive, miscellaneous, NBC, or AOV classes before being granted prechampionship, or provi-

sional breed, status. Cats in provisional breed competition are judged according to a provisional standard, but once their new breed gains full recognition, they become eligible for championship classes. The exotic shorthair bypassed this typical acceptance process when it was accepted as a new breed at a 1966 CFA Board of Directors meeting.

Showing Longhaired Exotics

All North American registries permit exotic outcross breedings to Persians and Himalayans, but their policies on registering and showing the inevitable percentage of longhaired offspring that result from these matings vary widely. For example, in TICA, the exotic is a member of the Persian/Himalayan/ Exotic Shorthair Breed Group. This means that these breeds can outcross to any of the others, and the longhaired kittens can be registered and shown as Persians or, if they are pointed, as Himalayans. UFO permits the longhaired exotics in the longhair class as a separate breed, and not as a division of either the exotic shorthairs or the Persians. ACFA and CFF also recog-

The judging ring: During a cat show class, a judge removes each cat from its cage and examines it on a table in front of interested onlookers.

Exotic shorthairs are currently recognized in all of the colors of the Persian cat, but bicolors like this beautiful blue and white exotic are especially popular now.

nize them separately as longhaired exotics. Similarly, ACA, AACE, and NCFA created a separate championship division for exotic longhairs and permit them to be registered as such. At this time, longhaired exotics can be shown only as AOVs in CFA, although efforts are underway to change this. In Europe, all registering organizations, including the Fédération Internationale Féline (FIFe), recognize longhaired exotics as Persians and allow them to be bred and shown as such.

Entering Your First Show

A good way to become involved in showing cats is to join a cat club in your area that is affiliated with one of the cat-registering associations. For club information and show rules, call or write the association(s) in which your cat is registered. Some registries charge a small fee to cover the cost of printing and mailing their rule booklets. The breeder of your cat should also be willing to help you get started, because

your wins in the show ring will reflect favorably on his or her bloodlines and cattery name.

If you're not involved with a club, check cat magazine show date listings, then write or call the number given for entry forms and information. Complete the entry form by the specified deadline and return it to the entry clerk along with the appropriate fee. You also may request to be "benched" next to your breeder or to someone you know who is an experienced exhibitor. Your "benching assignment" is the cage where your cat will stay when it's not being judged in one of the rings.

Cages and Supplies

The show flyer will list all pertinent information about the show, including the cage dimensions. Benching cages for a single cat are small, but for a little extra money, you may have the option of requesting a double cage on the entry form you submit. On the day of the show, you will need to bring some spray disinfectant to wipe down your cat's cage, plus fabric, towels, or show curtains to line the inside and bottom of the cage. Covering the cage gives your cat a little privacy amid the show hall noise and shields it from seeing the other cats in adjacent cages. This also adds an element of fun, because most shows have contests for the best decorated cage. Many exhibitors go all out to custom-design attractive cage curtains that effectively advertise their breed and catteries.

Generally, the show committee provides a chair at each cage, cat litter, and sometimes disposable litter boxes. You'll have to bring a small litter pan, just in case, plus your grooming equipment, a grooming table (a sturdy TV tray or plastic patio table serve the same purpose), a cat carrier, a cat bed, food and water bowls, your cat's favorite food, and any other accessories to make your cat feel comfortable. Of course, you will have completed most of your cat's grooming at home, having bathed it a day or two before the show. Only touch-ups should be required at the show, but be prepared, just in case your cat makes a major mess of its fur in transit.

"Vetting"

To enter the show hall, your cat must be flea-free and disease-free. In some countries, such as Great Britain, many shows are "vetted," meaning that a veterinarian screens each cat before it is allowed inside the show hall. Although U.S. shows do not require vetting, inoculations must be up-to-date. The show flyer will state whether you must bring proof of current vaccinations for rabies or other diseases.

Judging

After you check in at the door on the day of the show and get your cat settled in its assigned cage, read the catalog schedule to determine when your cat will be judged. Listen to the public address system, and when you hear your cat's number called, carry your cat to the appropriate judging ring. Your number will be posted on top of one of the cages in the ring. Place your cat in the correct cage, then take a seat in the audience to quietly watch the judging.

The judge will examine each cat in turn on the table and hang ribbons on the winners' cages at the end of the class. When the judging is over, the clerk will ask the exhibitors to remove their cats from the ring. Collect your cat and ribbons, if any, and return to your benching cage to await your call to the next ring. Depending on how well your cat does, it may be called back for finals, when the top contestants in a given category are presented. The highest awards at a show include Best of Breed and the most coveted prize, Best in Show. Cats that

The Exotic Shorthair breed standard calls for a cat that is heavily-boned but well balanced and that has a sweet expression and soft, round lines.

win in the championship or premiership finals earn points based on the number of cats defeated at the show. These points count toward regional and national titles. To understand the ribbons, points, and awards system more fully, consult the rules booklet prepared by the cat fancy association sponsoring the show.

Traveling with Your Exotic

Although your first cat show should be within driving distance of your home, traveling to the show may be a stressful ordeal for your exotic. Some cats enjoy riding in a car, but many do not. Some even get car sick. If you're going to show your exotic, get it accustomed to traveling in a car while still a kitten. Take it for short drives around the block every few days, gradually increasing the time spent in the car. For safety reasons, keep your cat in a pet carrier while traveling. This practice not only minimizes escape opportunities, but also prevents a frightened or exploring cat from getting under the gas and brake pedals or otherwise interfering with the driver's ability to control the car. Confining your exotic to a carrier lessens the likelihood of injury from being tossed about the vehicle and reduces the risk of escape through a broken car window, in case of an accident.

When packing, take along your cat's bed, a favorite toy, feeding bowls, food, and medications. It's also a good idea to take a gallon or two of water from home, or bottled water, because different drinking water can sometimes bring on a bout of diarrhea. The show flyer should recommend hotels that allow pets. If not, inquire in advance about the pet policy at the place where you plan to stay, and don't forget to take a litter box for use in the hotel room. If you must leave your cat alone in the hotel room for brief periods, put it in the carrier or in a children's play tent. These play tents are lightweight, easy to pack, and roomy enough for your cat, a litter pan, a pet bed, and food dishes. When you leave the room, hang out the DO NOT DISTURB sign. You don't want housekeeping personnel to enter while you're dining and let your cat accidentally slip out the door.

For long drives, set a litter box in the floor of the car and take along a harness and leash so you can let your cat out of its carrier for rest stops. Before opening the car door, secure your exotic in a carrier or on a leash. Because of the risk of heat stroke, never, *never* leave your exotic unattended in a parked car, especially on warm days (see First Aid for heat stroke, page 47).

Traveling by Air

If traveling to a show by air, make sure your cat carrier conforms to the airline's regulations. Many pet-travel accidents are a result of poorly constructed carriers. A standard shipping carrier should be made of metal, sturdy wood, fiberglass, or rigid plastic. One entire end must be open for ventilation and covered with metal bars or heavy wire. The remaining sides should have ventilation slots, and all ventilation slots or holes should be protected by protruding rims to prevent obstruction by other baggage. The door latch and joints of the container must be escape-proof and impervious to biting and clawing. The container must be clearly labeled with "Live Animal" and "This End Up" and tagged with the cat and owner's names and address, plus any feeding instructions.

Some airlines allow pets in the passenger cabin as carry-on luggage, but

Cat carriers used in air travel should be well-ventilated and built of sturdy materials.

they must remain in a special-size carrier that fits under the seat. Other airlines allow animals to be transported only in the cargo hold, and some offer special expedited delivery service for animals. Most require a health certificate issued by a veterinarian.

Although aircraft cargo holds are pressurized and temperature-controlled during flight, onboard hazards can arise during delays on the ground, before take-off and after touchdown, when the plane's compartments are not air pressurized. During that time, temperatures inside the cargo hold can fluctuate rapidly. Careful planning can help minimize these dangers when transporting an animal by air. Whenever possible, book a non-stop flight, avoid holiday or weekend travel, and avoid flying during excessively hot or cold periods. Also, when you board the plane, make sure the airline pilot knows that there is an animal in the cargo hold.

Although tranquilizers may relieve some of your cat's travel anxiety, drugs also may make an animal more susceptible to temperature changes and breathing problems. Because tranquilizers can have unpredictable side effects in some animals at high altitudes, use them only under the advice and guidance of a veterinarian.

Boarding Your Exotic

If you're taking one cat to a show but leaving another at home, ask a trusted friend or neighbor to look in on it, or consider hiring a pet sitter to care for it while you're away. Leaving your exotic in its normal environment is less traumatic than boarding it in unfamiliar surroundings at a kennel or a veterinarian's office. However, deviation from the normal household routine upsets some animals and may result in behavior problems, such as house soiling. If your exotic is subject to this behavior, it may be better off at a boarding facility, where it can be supervised. To lessen your exotic's separation anxiety, leave something with your scent on it (an unwashed T-shirt or house slipper) to comfort the cat while you're away.

If you decide to use a professional pet sitter or boarding kennel, ask friends for recommendations, and check out the operator's references and business credentials. Inspect a boarding facility's premises for cleanliness beforehand, and ask about provisions for your cat's security and comfort. Select a kennel that houses cats in an area separate from dogs. A reputable kennel will also require proof that animals are up-to-date on all inoculations. Some will automatically flea-dip the animal at the owner's expense when it is brought in to ensure that it doesn't have any fleas.

Whatever arrangements you choose to make, leave an itinerary of where you will be and how you can be reached. Also, be sure to leave your veterinarian's telephone number with the person tending to your cat. One obvious advantage of boarding your exotic at a veterinary hospital is that medically trained personnel are on hand to observe and handle any emergency illness your cat may experience while you're away.

Even if you're going away for several hours and leave out enough food and water in self-feeders for your cat, let someone know where you're going and when you'll be back. That someone also should have a key to your home and permission to enter and look after your cat in case you're involved in an accident that delays your return.

The Exotic Breed Standard

In the cat fancy world, a breed standard is a written blueprint describing the ideal conformation and coloring of animals representing a particular breed. Every cat competing in a show is judged according to how well it meets the written standard for its breed. For use in their breeding programs, conscientious breeders try to select cats that most closely fit the standard or that possess enough of the desired qualities to promise outstanding offspring.

Selective breeding sometimes results in new colors that may be added to the standard after meeting certain criteria. Policies for accepting new varieties and colors vary widely among the different cat-registering associations, and committees convene periodically to amend and update the standards. Breed standards in foreign countries sometimes accept colors or varieties not recognized in the United States and may vary in other ways as well. That's why, if you're interested in showing your purebred cat, it's important to write to the appropriate association(s) and request their most current information and show standards (see Useful Addresses and Literature, page 101).

CFA Exotic Show Standard (as of May 1996)

In the show ring, an exotic is judged on how closely it fits the ideal standard adopted by the association governing the show. Points are assigned for various features, with a total score of 100 possible, but rare. The chart on page 82 lists the CFA point scores allowed for exotics.

CFA's standard for exotics is included here because it is the world's largest registry of pedigreed cats.

For cats in the tabby division, the 20 points for color are to be divided 10 for markings and 10 for color. For cats in the bicolor division, the 20

Dilute calico van female exotic. The significance of a van-colored cat is that it is homozygous for the bicolor (white spotting or piebald) gene.

points for color are to be divided 10 for "with white" pattern and 10 for color.

General: The ideal exotic should present an impression of a heavily boned, well-balanced cat with a sweet expression and soft, round lines. The large, round eyes set wide apart in a large round head contribute to the overall look and expression. The thick, plush coat softens the lines of the cat and accentuates the roundness in appearance.

Head: Round and massive, with great breadth of skull. Round face with round underlying bone-structure. Well set on a short, thick neck.

Nose: Short, snub, and broad, with "break" centered between the eyes. (**Note**: The characteristic break is a noticeable "stop" in the profile between the forehead and the nose.)

Cheeks: Full.

Jaws: Broad and powerful.

Chin: Full, well-developed, and firmly rounded, reflecting a proper bite.

Ears: Small, round tipped, tilted forward, and not unduly open at the base. Set far apart, and low on the head, fitting into (without distorting) the rounded contour of the head.

Eyes: Brilliant in color, large, round, and full. Set level and far apart, giving a sweet expression to the face.

Body: Of cobby type, low on the legs, broad and deep through the chest, equally massive across the shoulders and rump, with a well-rounded mid-section and level back. Good muscle tone, with no evidence of obesity. Large or medium in size. Quality the determining consideration rather than size.

Legs: Short, thick, and strong. Forelegs straight.

Paws: Large, round, and firm. Toes carried close, five in front and four behind.

Tail: Short, but in proportion to body length. Carried without a curve and at an angle lower than the back.

Coat: Dense, plush, soft, and full of life. Standing out from the body due to a rich, thick undercoat. Medium in length. Acceptable length depends on proper undercoat. Cats with a ruff or tail-feathers (long hair on the tail) shall be transferred to the AOV class.

Disqualify: Locket or button. Kinked or abnormal tail. Incorrect number of toes. Any apparent weakness in the hindquarters. Any apparent deformity of the spine. Deformity of the skull resulting in an asymmetrical face and/or head. Crossed eyes. For pointed cats, disqualify for white toes, eye color other than blue.

CFA Show Standard Exotic Colors

White: Pure glistening white. Nose leather (the skin around the nostrils) and paw pads: pink. Eye color: deep blue or brilliant copper. Odd-eyed whites shall have one blue and one copper eye with equal color depth.

Blue: Blue, lighter shade preferred, one level tone from nose to tip of tail. A sound darker shade is more acceptable than an unsound lighter shade. Nose leather and paw pads: blue. Eye color: copper.

Black: Dense coal black, sound from roots to tip of fur. Free from any tinge of rust on tips or smoke undercoat. Nose leather: black. Paw pads: black or brown. Eye color: brilliant copper.

Red: Deep, rich, clear, brilliant red; without shading, markings, or ticking. Lips and chin the same color as coat. Nose leather and paw pads: brick red. Eye color: brilliant copper.

Peke-faced Red: The peke-face cat should conform in color and general type to the standard set forth for the red cat; however, allowance should be made for the slightly higher placement of the ears to conform with the underlying bone structure of the head, which differs greatly from that of the standard exotic. The nose should be short, depressed, and indented between the eyes. The muzzle should be wrinkled. Eyes should be large, round, and set wide apart. The horizontal break, which is located between the usual nose break and the top dome of the head, runs straight across the front of the head creating half-moon boning above the eyes and an additional horizontal indentation located in the center of the forehead bone structure. This bone structure results in a very round head with a strong chin. Eye color: brilliant copper.

Cream: One level shade of buff cream, without markings, sound to the roots. Lighter shades preferred. Nose leather and paw pads: pink. Eye color: brilliant copper.

Chocolate: Rich, warm chocolate-brown, sound from roots to tip of fur. Nose leather and paw pads: cinnamon-pink. Eye color: brilliant copper.

Lilac: Rich, warm lavender with a pinkish tone, sound and even throughout. Nose leather and paw pads: lavender-pink. Eye color: brilliant copper.

Chinchilla Silver: Undercoat pure white. Coat on back, flanks, head, and tail sufficiently tipped with black to give the characteristic sparkling silver appearance. Legs may be slightly shaded with tipping. Chin, ear tufts, stomach, and chest, pure white. Rims of eyes, lips, and nose outlined with black. Nose leather: brick red. Paw pads: black. Eye color: green or blue-green. Disqualify (silvers and goldens) for incorrect eye color, incorrect eye color being copper, yellow, gold, amber, or any color other than green or blue-green.

Shaded Silver: Undercoat white with a mantle of black tipping shading down from sides, face, and tail from dark on the ridge to white on the chin, chest, stomach, and under the tail. Rims of eyes, lips, and nose outlined with black. Nose leather: brick red. Paw pads: black. Eye color: green or blue-green.

Chinchilla Golden: Undercoat rich warm cream. Coat on back, flanks, head, and tail sufficiently tipped with black to give golden appearance. Legs may be slightly shaded with tipping. Chin, ear tufts, stomach, and chest, cream. Rims of eyes, lips, and nose outlined with black. Nose leather: deep rose. Paw pads: black. Eye color: green or blue-green.

Shaded Golden: Undercoat rich warm cream with a mantle of black tipping shading down from the sides, face, and tail from dark on the ridge to cream on the chin, chest, stomach, and under the tail. Legs to be the same tone as the face. The general effect to be much darker than a chinchilla. Rims of eyes, lips, and nose outlined with black. Nose leather: deep rose. Paw pads: black. Eye color: green or blue-green.

Shell Cameo (Red Chinchilla): Undercoat white, the coat on the back, flanks, head, and tail to be sufficiently tipped with red to give the characteristic sparkling appearance. Face and legs may be very slightly shaded with tipping. Chin, ear tufts, stomach, and chest, white on the chin, chest, stomach, and under the tail. Nose leather, rims of eyes, and paw pads: rose. Eye color: brilliant copper.

Shaded Cameo (Red Shaded): Undercoat white with a mantle of red tipping shading down the sides, face, and tail from dark on the ridge to white on the chin, chest, stomach, and under the tail. Nose leather, rims of eyes, and paw pads: rose. Eye color: brilliant copper.

Cream Shell Cameo (Cream Chinchilla): Undercoat white. Coat on back, flanks, head, and tail sufficiently tipped with cream to give the characteristic sparkling appearance. Face and legs may be slightly shaded with tipping. Chin, ear tufts, stomach, and chest, white. Nose leather and paw pads: pink. Eye color: brilliant copper.

Cream Shaded Cameo (Cream Shaded): Undercoat white with a mantle of cream tipping shading down from sides, face, and tail from dark on the ridge to white on the chin, chest, stomach, and under the tail. Nose leather and paw pads: pink. Eye color: brilliant copper.

Shell Tortoiseshell: Undercoat white. Coat on the back, flanks, head, and tail to be delicately tipped in black with well-defined patches of red and cream tipped hairs as in the pattern of the tortoiseshell. Face and legs may be slightly shaded with tipping. Chin, ear tufts, stomach, and chest, white to very slightly tipped. Blaze of red or cream tipping on face is desirable. Eye color: brilliant copper.

Shaded Tortoiseshell: Undercoat white. Mantle of black tipping and clearly defined patches of red and cream tipped hairs as in the pattern of the tortoiseshell. Shading down the sides, face, and tail from dark on the ridge to slightly tipped or white on the chin, chest, stomach, legs, and under the tail.

Shell Blue-cream (Blue-cream Chinchilla): Undercoat white. Coat on back, flanks, head and tail to be delicately tipped in blue with patches of cream tipped hairs as in the pattern of the blue-cream. Face and legs may be slightly shaded with tipping. Chin, ear tufts, stomach, and chest, white. Nose leather and paw pads: blue and/or pink. Eye color: brilliant copper.

Shaded Blue-cream: Undercoat white. Mantle of blue tipping with patches of cream tipped hairs as in the pattern of blue-cream, shading down from sides, face, and tail from dark on the ridge to white on the chin, chest, stomach, and under the tail. Nose leather and paw pads: blue and/or pink. Eye color: brilliant copper.

Black Smoke: White undercoat, deeply tipped with black. Cat in repose appears black. In motion the white undercoat is clearly apparent. Light silver frill and ear tufts. Nose leather and paw pads: black. Eye color: brilliant copper.

Blue Smoke: White undercoat, deeply tipped with blue. Cat in repose appears blue. In motion the white undercoat is clearly apparent. White frill and ear tufts. Nose leather and paw pads: blue. Eye color: brilliant copper.

Cream Smoke: White undercoat, deeply tipped with cream. Cat in repose appears cream. In motion the white undercoat is clearly apparent. Nose leather and paw pads: pink. Eye color: brilliant copper.

Cameo Smoke (Red Smoke): White undercoat, deeply tipped with red. Cat in repose appears red. In motion the white undercoat is clearly apparent. Nose leather, rims of eyes, and paw pads: rose. Eye color: brilliant copper.

Tortoiseshell Smoke: White undercoat, deeply tipped with black with clearly defined unbrindled patches of red and cream tipped hairs as in the pattern of the tortoiseshell. (**Note:** The term "unbrindled" means the colored area has no intermingling, obscure streaks or flecks of another color.) Cat

The exotic's characteristic nose "break" is a noticeable stop in the facial profile between the nose and forehead.

in repose appears tortoiseshell. In motion the white undercoat is clearly apparent. White ruff and ear tufts. Blaze of red or cream tipping on face is desirable. Eye color: brilliant copper.

Blue-cream Smoke: White undercoat deeply tipped with blue, with clearly defined patches of cream as in

White exotics can have one blue eye and one copper eye, giving them a striking appearance, like this attractive odd-eyed youngster.

the pattern of the blue-cream. Cat in repose appears blue-cream. In motion the white undercoat is clearly apparent. Eye color: copper.

Classic Tabby Pattern: Markings dense, clearly defined, and broad. Legs evenly barred with bracelets coming up to meet the body markings. Tail evenly ringed. Several unbroken necklaces on neck and upper chest, the more the better. Frown marks on forehead form an intricate letter "M." Unbroken line runs back from outer corner of eye. Swirls on cheeks. Vertical lines over back of head extend to shoulder markings that are in the shape of a butterfly with both upper and lower wings distinctly outlined and marked with dots inside outline. Back markings consist of a vertical line down the spine from butterfly to tail with a vertical stripe paralleling it on each side, the three stripes well separated by stripes of the ground color. Large solid blotch on each side to be encircled by one or more unbroken rings. Side markings should be the same on both sides. Double vertical rows of buttons on chest and stomach.

Mackerel Tabby Pattern: Markings dense, clearly defined, and all narrow pencilings. Legs evenly barred with narrow bracelets coming up to meet the body markings. Tail barred. Necklaces on neck and chest distinct, like so many chains. Head barred with an "M" on the forehead. Unbroken lines running back from the eyes. Lines running down the head to meet the shoulders. Spine lines run together to form a narrow saddle. Narrow pencilings run around body.

Silver Tabby (Classic, Mackerel): Ground color pale, clear silver. Markings dense black. Undercoat white. Lips and chin the same shade as the rings around the eyes. Nose leather: brick red. Paw pads: black. Eye color: green, hazel, or copper.

Silver Patched Tabby (Classic, Mackerel): Ground color pale silver. Markings of dense black. Patches of red or softly intermingled areas of red on both body and extremities. Undercoat white. Nose leather: brick red. Paw pads: black and/or brick red. Eye color: green, hazel, or brilliant copper.

Blue Silver Tabby (Classic, Mackerel): Ground color pale bluish silver. Markings sound blue. Undercoat white. Nose leather: blue or old rose trimmed with blue. Paw pads: blue or old rose. Eye color: green, hazel, or brilliant copper.

Blue Silver Patched Tabby (Classic, Mackerel): Ground color pale bluish silver. Markings sound blue. Patches of cream or softly inter-mingled areas of cream on both body and extremities. Undercoat white. Lips and chin the same shade as the rings around the eyes. Nose leather: blue or old rose trimmed with blue and/or pink. Paw pads: blue or old rose and/or pink. Eye color: green, hazel, or brilliant copper.

Red Tabby (Classic, Mackerel): Ground color red. Markings deep, rich red. Nose leather and paw pads: brick red. Eye color: brilliant copper.

Peke-face Red Tabby (Classic, Mackerel): The peke-face cat should conform in color and general type to the standard set forth for the red tabby cat; however, allowance should be made for the slightly higher placement of the ears to conform with the underlying bone structure of the head, which differs greatly from that of the standard exotic. The nose should be short, depressed, and indented between the eyes. The muzzle should be wrinkled. Eyes should be large, round, and set wide apart. The horizontal break, which is located between the usual nose break and the top dome of the head, runs straight across the front of the head creating half-moon boning above the eyes and an additional hori-

Tortoiseshell exotic shorthair.

zontal indentation located in the center of the forehead bone structure. This bone structure results in a very round head with a strong chin. Eye color: brilliant copper.

Brown Tabby (Classic, Mackerel): Ground color brilliant coppery brown. Markings dense black. Lips and chin the same shade as the rings around the eyes. Back of leg black from paw to heel. Nose leather: brick red. Paw pads: black or brown. Eye color: brilliant copper.

Blue McTabby and white exotic shorthair.

Brown Patched Tabby (Classic, Mackerel): Ground color brilliant coppery brown. Markings of dense black. Patches of red or softly intermingled areas of red on both body and extremities. Nose leather: brick red. Paw pads: black and/or brick red. Eye color: brilliant copper.

Blue Tabby (Classic, Mackerel): Ground color, including lips and chin, pale bluish ivory. Markings a very deep blue affording a good contrast with ground color. Warm fawn overtones or patina over the whole. Nose leather: old rose. Paw pads: rose. Eye color: brilliant copper.

Blue Patched Tabby (Classic, Mackerel): Ground color pale bluish ivory. Markings of very deep blue affording a good contrast with ground color. Patches of cream or softly intermingled areas of cream on both body and extremities. Warm fawn overtones or patina over the whole. Nose leather: old rose and/or pink. Paw pads: rose and/or pink. Eye color: brilliant copper.

Cream Tabby (Classic, Mackerel): Ground color pale cream. Markings of buff or cream sufficiently darker than the ground color to afford good contrast, but remaining within the dilute color range. Nose leather and paw pads: pink. Eye color: brilliant copper.

Cameo Tabby (Classic, Mackerel): Ground color off-white. Markings red. Undercoat white. Lips and chin the same shade as the rings around the eyes. Nose leather and paw pads: pink. Eye color: brilliant copper.

Cream Cameo Tabby (Classic, Mackerel): Ground color off-white. Markings cream. Undercoat white. Nose leather and paw pads: pink. Eye color: copper.

Tortoiseshell: Black with patches of red or softly intermingled areas of red on both body and extremities. Presence of several shades of red acceptable. Nose leather and paw

pads: black and/or brick red. Eye color: brilliant copper.

Blue-cream: Blue with patches of cream or softly intermingled areas of cream on both body and extremities. Lighter shades preferred. Nose leather and paw pads: blue and/or pink. Eye color: brilliant copper.

Chocolate Tortoiseshell: Rich, warm chocolate brown with patches of red or softly intermingled areas of red on both body and extremities. Nose leather and paw pads: brown and/or brick red. Eye color: brilliant copper.

Lilac-cream: Rich, warm pinkish toned lavender with patches of cream or softly intermingled areas of cream on both body and extremities. Nose leather and paw pads: pink. Eye color: brilliant copper.

Calico: White with unbrindled patches of black and red. As a preferred minimum, the cat should have white feet, legs, undersides, chest, and muzzle. Less white than this minimum should be penalized proportionately. Inverted "V" blaze on face desirable. Eye color: brilliant copper.

Van Calico: White cat with unbrindled patches of black and red confined to the extremities, head, tail, and legs. One or two small colored patches on body allowable. Eye color: brilliant copper.

Dilute Calico: White with unbrindled patches of blue and cream. Eye color: brilliant copper.

Van Dilute Calico: White cat with unbrindled patches of blue and cream confined to the extremities, head, tail, and legs. Eye color: copper.

Chocolate Calico: White with unbrindled patches of chocolate and red. Nose leather and paw pads: brown, brick red, and/or pink. Eye color: brilliant copper.

Chocolate Van Calico: White cat with unbrindled patches of chocolate and red confined to the extremities, head, tail, and legs. Nose leather and paw pads: brown, brick red, and/or pink. Eye color: brilliant copper.

Lilac Calico: White with unbrindled patches of lilac and cream. As a preferred minimum, the cat should have white feet, legs, undersides, chest, and muzzle. Nose leather and paw pads: pink. Eye color: brilliant copper.

Lilac Van Calico: White cat with unbrindled patches of lilac and cream confined to the extremities, head, tail, and legs. Nose leather and paw pads: pink. Eye color: brilliant copper.

Bicolor: Black and white, blue and white, red and white, cream and white, chocolate and white, or lilac and white. As a preferred minimum, the cat should have white feet, legs, undersides, chest, and muzzle. Less white than this minimum should be penalized proportionately. Inverted "V" blaze on face desirable. Eye color: brilliant copper.

Van Bicolor: Black and white, red and white, blue and white, cream and white, chocolate and white, or lilac and white. White cat with color confined to the extremities, head, tail, and legs. One or two small colored patches on body allowable. Eye color: brilliant copper.

Smoke and White: White with colored portions, the colored portions of the cat to conform to the currently established smoke color standards. Eye color: brilliant copper.

Van Smoke and White: White cat with colored portions confined to the extremities, head, tail, and legs. The colored portions conform to the currently established smoke color standards. Eye color: brilliant copper.

Tabby and White: White with colored portions that conform to the currently established classic, mackerel and patched tabby color standards.

Van Tabby and White: White cat with tabby coloring confined to the extremities, head, tail, and legs.

Himalayan (Point) Pattern: Body color even, with subtle shading when allowed. Points: mask, ears, legs, feet, and tail color dense and clearly defined, all of the same shade. Mask covers entire face including whisker pads and chin, but no further back than front of ears. There must be a definite contrast between body color and point color.

Chocolate Point: Body ivory with no shading. Points milk-chocolate color, warm in tone. Nose leather and paw pads: cinnamon pink. Eye color: deep vivid blue.

Seal Point: Body even pale fawn to cream, warm in tone, shading gradually into lighter color on the stomach and chest. Points deep seal brown. Nose leather and paw pads: seal brown. Eye color: deep vivid blue.

Lilac Point: Body glacial white with no shading. Points frosty gray with pinkish tone. Nose leather and paw pads: lavender pink. Eye color: blue.

Blue Point: Body bluish white, cold in tone, shading gradually to white on stomach and chest. Points blue. Nose leather and paw pads: slate blue. Eye color: deep vivid blue.

Red Point: Body creamy white. Points deep orange flame to deep red. Nose leather and paw pads: flesh to coral pink. Eye color: deep vivid blue.

Cream Point: Body creamy white with no shading. Points buff cream with no apricot. Nose leather and paw pads: flesh to coral pink. Eye color: deep vivid blue.

Tortie Point: Body creamy white or pale fawn. Points seal with unbrindled patches of red and/or cream. Blaze of red or cream on face is desirable. Nose leather and paw pads: seal brown and/or coral pink. Eye color: deep vivid blue.

Blue-cream Point: Body bluish white or creamy white, shading gradually to white on the stomach and chest. Points blue with patches

Cream and white exotic shorthair.

of cream. Nose leather and paw pads: slate blue and/or pink. Eye color: blue.

Chocolate-Tortie Point: Body ivory with no shading. Points chocolate with unbrindled patches of red and/or cream. Nose leather and paw pads: cinnamon pink and/or coral pink. Eye color: deep vivid blue.

Lilac-cream Point: body glacial white with no shading. Points lilac with patches of cream. Nose leather and paw pads: lavender pink and/or pink. Eye color: deep vivid blue.

Himalayan Lynx (Point) Pattern: Mask must be clearly lined with dark stripes, vertical and forming the classic "M" on the forehead; horizontal on the cheeks. The mask contains light rings around the eyes and dark spots on light whisker pads, clearly outlined in dark color edges. Inner ear light with ticking on outer ear. Markings dense, clearly defined and broad. Legs evenly barred with bracelets. Tail barred with

Brown tabby exotic shorthair.

lighter underside. No striping or mottling on body.

Seal Lynx Point: Points beige-brown ticked with darker brown tabby markings. Body color pale cream to fawn, warm in tone. Nose leather: seal brown or brick red. Paw pads: seal brown. Eye color: deep vivid blue.

Blue Lynx Point: Points light, silvery blue, ticked with darker blue tabby markings. Body color bluish white, cold in tone. Nose leather: blue or old rose. Paw pads: blue. Eye color: deep vivid blue.

Red Lynx Point: Points deep orange flame ticked with deep red tabby markings. Body color creamy white. Nose leather and paw pads: flesh to coral pink. Eye color: blue.

Cream Lynx Point: Points pale cream ticked with dark cream tabby markings. Body color creamy white, significantly lighter in tone than the points. Nose leather and paw pads: flesh to coral pink. Eye color: blue.

Blue patched tabby and white exotic shorthair.

Red and white exotic shorthair.

Tortie Lynx Point: Points beige-brown with dark brown tabby markings and patches of red. Body color creamy white or pale fawn. Nose leather and paw pads: seal brown, brick red, and/or coral pink. Eye color: deep vivid blue.

Blue-cream Lynx Point: Points blue with darker blue tabby markings and patches of cream. Body color bluish white, cold in tone. Nose leather and paw pads: blue, old rose, and/or pink. Eye color: deep vivid blue.

Chocolate Lynx Point: Points milk-chocolate ticked with darker chocolate tabby markings. Body color ivory. Nose leather and paw pads: cinnamon pink or coral pink. Eye color: deep vivid blue.

Lilac Lynx Point: Points pale frosty gray with pinkish tone ticked with darker lilac tabby markings. Body color glacial white. Nose leather and paw pads: lavender pink. Eye color: blue.

Chocolate-Tortie Lynx Point: Points milk-chocolate ticked with darker chocolate tabby markings and patches of red. Body color ivory. Nose leather and paw pads: cinnamon pink and/or coral pink. Eye color: blue.

Lilac-cream Lynx Point: Points pale frosty gray with pinkish tone ticked with darker lilac tabby markings and patches of cream. Body color glacial white. Nose leather and paw pads: lavender pink and/or coral pink. Eye color: deep vivid blue. (*Source: The Cat Fanciers Association, Exotic Show Standard and Exotic Colors, May, 1996.*)

Breeding Your Exotic

Hard to Breed

Breeding exotics can be especially frustrating, because about half of the kittens will have long hair if both parents possess the recessive longhair gene. Particularly disheartening is the reality that breeding exotic to exotic tends to increase the number of short-haired kittens while sacrificing the ideal plush coat and Persian body type. Breeding back to the Persian periodically seems necessary to maintain these attributes, but it also keeps that recessive longhair gene in the pool.

Aside from the genetic considerations, breeding purebred exotic cats is an expensive, labor-intensive hobby. Stud fees average about $500, depending on the male's quality, color, and show record. If the stud is a grand champion or a national winner, you can count on the fee being much higher. Figure in the travel costs of transporting your female cat to the stud for breeding, the veterinary bills, vaccinations, cat food, advertising expenses, etc., and you can quickly see how little one profits from raising a litter of kittens.

Even after writing off allowable expenses on their business taxes, most professional breeders consider themselves lucky if they break even. To them, the real "profits" in breeding are intangible achievements, such as a Best in Show rosette, regional and national awards, and the respect of fellow cat fanciers who recognize their contributions to the exotic breed. If these aspirations do not interest you, leave breeding to the professionals.

Concentrate, instead, on being the best-educated pet owner you can be, and share your knowledge with others. Read books about cats. Subscribe to cat magazines. Volunteer at your local animal shelter. Set an example as a responsible cat owner.

Rather than breeding your cat so that your children can witness the "miracle of birth," show them how to take responsibility for the animals already in this world by teaching them how proper health care, spaying, and neutering can reduce the suffering that more than eight million surplus pets endure each year. That's how many animals wind up abused, neglected, and homeless in U.S. shelters every year. Most must be humanely destroyed because there simply aren't enough homes to go around for so many. The way to reduce this senseless waste of life is to end all indiscriminate breeding by spaying and neutering pets and by *never* allowing intact animals to roam freely.

Getting Started as a Serious Breeder

Before you start breeding cats, acquire an altered exotic and learn all about show ring competition. Memorize the show standard; talk to cat show judges and other breeders so that you understand what features make an exotic a good show cat. Join a cat club in your area. Then, If you're still determined to get seriously involved in breeding, despite the expense, hard work, and (often) heartbreak involved, acquire the best quality exotic female you can afford. Or, find an experienced breeder who is willing to co-own breeding stock with you while you learn.

Breeding exotics can be frustrating because about half of the kittens in a litter will be born with long hair.

As a serious breeder, consider it your duty to place the kittens you produce in loving homes. Make sure that all pet-quality animals you place get spayed or neutered by their new owners, or elect to have them altered yourself at an early age, before they go to new homes.

Breeding Complications

Breeding purebred cats is not without problems. For health reasons, a female should be bred only once—certainly no more than twice—a year. Expect your feed costs to climb, because the queen will need extra protein and high-quality rations while she is pregnant and nursing. Inadequate nutrition could result in the loss of kittens, and perhaps even the queen. Other complications also can occur.

Cesarean Sections

Because of the large, round heads and big bone structure of their kittens, exotic queens tend to require cesarean sections more often than some other breeds. The operation, which opens the abdomen to deliver kittens, costs about $250, depending on your geographic location. Watch

the queen closely during delivery, and if she fails to produce a kitten after about an hour of hard labor, or if she is obviously in distress, seek veterinary help immediately. Do not wait until she is too exhausted to continue. Allowing her condition to weaken only increases the risks for her and her kittens, should a c-section become necessary.

Neonatal Isoerythrolysis (NI)

Occasional litters experience fading kitten syndrome after birth, an often-fatal condition resulting from mating individuals with incompatible blood types. This hemolytic reaction, called neonatal isoerythrolysis (NI), occurs when kittens that inherit blood-type A nurse from a mother with blood-type B. Type B kittens born to type A mothers are not prone to NI, because type A cats possess weaker anti-B antibodies. Blood-type B individuals, however, can have powerful antibodies against type A, and those antibodies present in the queen's colostrum (first milk) can destroy the type A kittens' red blood cells. These kittens appear healthy at birth, but they weaken and die soon afterward. You can attempt to save the kittens by removing them from the mother and hand-raising them, but fostering is a grueling commitment that requires frequent, round-the-clock feedings. To prevent NI, breed type B females only to type B males. Specialized tests can identify feline blood types. Cats have three known blood types—A, B, and AB, with A the most common and AB the most rare. Research indicates that type B occurs more often in certain purebreds, such as the Persian, than in mixed breeds.

Arranging Stud Service

When selecting a suitable stud, ask to see the male's pedigree and make sure he's a registered purebred. Whether you're breeding exotic to exotic or exotic to Persian, you want the male to be a champion or a grand champion and preferably a proven stud that has passed on his good qualities to previous litters. If he comes from a line of champions or grand champions, those cats' names will be prefixed by Ch. or Gr. Ch. on the pedigree. Choose a male that possesses the personality traits and/or physical qualities you would like to see enhanced in your female.

The written contract should state the agreed upon stud fee and the responsibilities of the stud owner while the female is housed in his or her cattery. Both parties should ask to see health certificates that prove their cats are vaccinated and free of feline leukemia virus and feline AIDS. Both cats also need to be free of fleas and other parasites before they are introduced for mating.

A conscientious exotic breeder may rightfully elect to withhold the registration papers of kittens sold as pets until they've been spayed or neutered.

The Feline Facts of Life

A breeding female cat is called a *queen*. An intact male is called a *tom* or *stud*. Ideally, a queen should not be bred until she is at least one year old, although her first heat cycle (estrus) may occur months earlier. Waiting a year allows the queen to achieve her full growth first, before essential nutrients must be diverted to nourish unborn kittens. A tom reaches sexual maturity between nine and 14 months, and from then on, his hormones drive him relentlessly to search for mates and to defend his territory against intruding toms. His sex hormones trigger his instinctive urge to spray and mark his territory with strong-smelling urine, which is one reason why a breeding male in a cattery typically is confined to a cage or spacious run. Neutering usually curbs this undesirable male trait, unless the habit has become well-established.

The Heat Cycle

A queen comes into heat according to seasonal rhythms, usually in early spring, mid-summer, and early fall. Feline reproductive cycles appear to be influenced by lengthening daylight hours, which explains why cats in the Northern Hemisphere cycle opposite to those in the southern half of the world. Most queens have heat cycles every two or three weeks during the breeding seasons; others cycle only once a month. There are many exceptions, and some cats living indoors in controlled, artificial lighting may cycle year-round.

A few queens have "silent" heats, but generally there's no mistaking when females come into season. The hallmark signs include increased restlessness and vocal calling. The queen may seem more affectionate toward her owners, rubbing against them and wanting to be petted. She may roll on the ground or pace from door to door. Take care to keep her in; if she escapes outdoors, she may mate with more than one male and deliver a mixed litter of kittens having different fathers. The most obvious and nerve-wracking behavior at this stage is known as the "call"—the queen's persistent, drawn-out, throaty howl that advertises her availability to the neighborhood toms. In response to this calling, plus the high levels of sex pheromones the queen's body produces, yowling toms from near and far line up on the fence ready to prove their worthiness as mates.

Also at this stage, the queen may crouch in the characteristic mating stance, called the *estrus* or *lordotic* posture. She will assume this posture, too, if you stroke her back near the base of the tail. With front end pressed to the ground and with back hollowed, she will raise her hindquarters, swish her tail to one side, and tread up and down with her hind feet, as if marching in place. If the queen is bred and becomes pregnant, gestation normally lasts an average 65 or 66 days. If mating does not take place, she enters a stage of sexual inactivity until her next cycle begins.

When your queen's behavior indicates that she is ready to mate, transport her to the stud. Unfortunately, traveling to strange surroundings sometimes causes a female to go out of heat, so you may have to leave her with the stud for an extended time or make more than one trip to achieve a successful mating. Generally, if the first mating fails, a second attempt with the same stud is free.

The Sex Act

When all goes according to nature's plan, the queen rolls provocatively for her suitor and assumes the mating stance, inviting the tom to mount her. The tom seizes her by the scruff of the neck and proceeds to pedal with his hind legs. The brief coupling ends with a howl and a hiss from the queen as the tom withdraws. Often, she turns to swat him with her paw. The two go off by themselves momentarily to groom or to watch one another, but soon they will rejoin and repeat the mating sequence many more times.

Induced Ovulation

Female cats are unusual in that they, unlike most other mammals, do not ovulate spontaneously during their cycles. Instead, they are "induced ovulators," meaning that the sex act must occur, usually repeatedly, to induce the release of eggs from the ovaries. To accomplish this, the male's penis is ridged with tiny spines or barbs that scrape the inside of the queen's vagina during copulation. This physical stimulation apparently sends a message along nerve pathways to areas in the brain that release luteinizing hormone, a chemical that prompts ovulation.

Signs of Pregnancy

About three weeks after conception, the queen's nipples redden or "pink up." Her attitude may become more maternal and affectionate. Her appetite may increase, and she will gradually put on a few extra pounds. Proper nutrition is vital for the queen's health and for the developing fetuses. Your veterinarian can recommend a cat food specially formulated for reproductive needs.

Cats, like people, can suffer from morning sickness due to hormonal changes. The queen may vomit occasionally during her third or fourth week, but the problem usually lasts only a few days and requires no veterinary treatment unless it becomes severe. Report any other signs of illness to your veterinarian immediately.

The queen's abdomen becomes noticeably swollen in about a month. Resist the temptation to palpate the kittens inside, as they or the distended uterus can be injured easily. Leave this inspection to your veterinarian. For the same reason, do not allow children to pick up the queen during her pregnancy.

Basic Feline Genetics

Genetics is the science of inheritance. Exotic parents pass on their breed characteristics and their individual qualities to the next generation of kittens via the genetic code contained in coiled strands called chromosomes. All body cells, except sperm and eggs, contain these chromosomes arranged in pairs. Cats have 19 pairs per cell, or 38 total. The sex cells, however, contain 19 single, unpaired chromosomes. When egg and sperm cells unite to form a new individual, the chromosomes pair up again to total 38, bringing half of the genetic code from the father and half from the mother.

The queen signals her readiness to mate by assuming the characteristic mating stance, called the estrus *or* lordotic *posture. The tom mounts the queen and typically bites the scruff of her neck. Coitus lasts only a few seconds.*

Genes

Chromosomes are made of a molecular material, called DNA (deoxyribonucleic acid), that carries the genetic code for how a kitten will look and behave. Bits of this code, such as eye color and coat length, are stored in smaller heredity units called *genes*. Genes are often called the building blocks of life because thousands of them, lined up along the chromosome strand, spell out the genetic blueprint for the entire animal. Most traits in the animal are produced by the complex organization and dynamic interaction of numerous genes. In some cases, a single gene can influence more than one trait.

Occasionally, a random change in the genetic blueprint causes a mutation in the individual that inherits the altered gene. Some mutations are bad, but others may benefit an individual by enabling it to adapt and survive better in its environment.

Because chromosomes are paired, genes for specific traits also are paired, one from each parent. This random sharing and pairing of genetic material from both parents is what allows species members to enjoy such remarkable diversity and individuality.

Alleles

Paired genes are also called *alleles*, and the gene that expresses its coded trait is said to be *dominant*. The other is *recessive*. Recessive genes can express their coded traits only when paired. For example, the gene that gives the exotic its short coat is dominant, while the gene that produces the Persian's long coat is recessive. If a kitten inherits a shorthair gene from one parent and a longhair gene from its other parent, it will have short fur, because the shorthair gene is dominant.

Color Inheritance

Some colors and markings are produced by recessive genes, while oth-

Every purebred exotic represents a substantial investment of time and money on the part of the breeder.

stood. The genetics of white spotting in cats also is not completely understood, due to the many unusual variations.

Gender

The sex chromosomes determine whether the cat will be a male or a female. All females have two sex chromosomes labeled XX; males have two sex chromosomes labeled XY. When these chromosomes pair up, one from each parent, to create a new individual, an X from the mother combined with an X from the father produces a female (XX) kitten. A male (XY) kitten results if the mother's X chromosome pairs with the Y from the father. Because only males possess the Y chromosome, the father determines each kitten's sex. Besides determining gender, sex chromosomes also can carry genes for other traits, and such traits are said to be sex-linked.

Certain colors, such as red (also called orange) are sex-linked traits carried on the X chromosome. Tortoiseshell, blue-cream, and calico cats are nearly always female.

ers, generally the more common ones, are produced by dominant genes. Some coat colors are paired with other traits, such as the blue eyes that accompany the pointed patterns. Similarly, the association of deafness with blue-eyed white cats is well-known, although not as well under-

Breeding Strategies

Breeders attempt to concentrate a cat's good qualities by breeding it to related cats that likely carry the same desirable genes. Unfortunately, inbreeding mother to son, father to daughter, etc., concentrates any bad qualities present in the family bloodline along with the good. *Linebreeding*, or mating distant relatives, achieves similar results, but often with fewer detrimental effects. Frequent outcrossing to separate bloodlines of the same breed helps keep the gene pool healthy and vigorous. Where permitted by the cat fancy's governing bodies, crossbreeding, or mating cats of different breeds, can be used to increase the gene pool or to create new breeds and colors.

The color white in the exotic is produced by a dominant gene.

Raising and Selling Exotics

Preparing for Birth

The average length of pregnancy in the cat is 65 or 66 days. After breeding your queen, make a note on your calendar, a week or so before the expected delivery date, to have a veterinarian examine her to ensure that all is well.

The entire time the queen is pregnant, and later while she is nursing, feed her a high-protein, high-quality feline growth and reproduction formula. Her protein needs will increase dramatically during the second half of her pregnancy, so follow your veterinarian's feeding guidelines. Also, unless directed by your veterinarian, avoid giving medications to your queen or using flea preparations on her while she is pregnant and nursing. Keep her indoors, especially during the last few weeks of pregnancy.

The Kittening Box

To prepare for the birth, make a kittening box for the queen to nest in. This can be a large cardboard or wooden box with a cut-out doorway and removable lid. Line the box bottom with old, clean towels, and place it in a warm, secluded, draft-free area, away from other pets and distracting noises. As the due date draws near, the queen's natural instincts will instruct her to rummage in closets and hideaways, looking for a suitable nesting site. When you notice this activity, show her the box, and she likely will figure out its intended purpose.

Supplies for the Birth

Some supplies to assemble before the delivery include:
• a heating pad or hot water bottle for warming the nest
• an antiseptic solution for treating the umbilical stumps
• scissors for cutting cords
• a hemostat for clamping cords or unwaxed dental floss (or thick cotton thread) for tying cords.

Delivering Kittens

At labor's onset, the queen may pant, cry loudly, and appear restless. She may go to the litter box and appear to strain, perhaps confusing

The kittening box can be made of wood, or you can use an ordinary cardboard container with lid flaps and an opening cut in one side. After she gives birth, the queen will need her food and water dishes and a litter box nearby.

Most queens will instinctively strip away the amniotic sac, sever the umbilical cord, and lick the kitten to stimulate its breathing. But keep a watchful eye out, and be prepared to step in and assist if necessary.

her contractions with the urge to eliminate. Talk to the queen reassuringly and minimize noise and distractions around her. If she seems upset by your hovering presence, observe her progress from a respectful distance. But do not leave her alone until all kittens are safely delivered. If complications arise, she will need your help.

If a kitten isn't breathing, grasp it securely in both hands and sling it upside down in a wide arc. This helps clear fluid from the respiratory passages.

The queen may crouch or lie on her side. She may sit up frequently to lick her vulva. When the contractions become more forceful, birth is imminent. You may see some fluid discharge as the water sac around the first kitten ruptures, lubricating its passage through the birth canal. From here on, things move rapidly, with kittens arriving about 15 to 30 minutes apart in most cases, although this can vary.

Presentation: About half of all kittens arrive head-first; the other half emerge hind feet and tail end first. This tail-first presentation is no cause for alarm unless you see the kitten's bottom but no feet. This means the hind legs are folded toward the head and is a true breech presentation that could complicate delivery. Call your veterinarian immediately.

Amniotic sac: Each kitten emerges either completely or partially enclosed in a grayish, semitransparent bubble, called the amniotic sac or placental membrane. Most experienced queens will instinctively strip this sac away, sever the umbilical cords, and forcefully lick each kitten clean to stimulate its breathing and circulation. A maiden queen having her first litter may not know what to do, so be prepared to assist by gently pinching the sac open and wiping mucous from the kitten's nose and mouth so it can breathe.

Umbilical cord: If the kitten is breathing and wriggling, there's no rush to cut the umbilical cord. Blood passes through the cord to the kitten from the placenta. When this blood flow stops, the cord constricts. If the queen gets busy delivering another kitten and neglects to chew through the cord, simply clamp or tie it one or two inches from the kitten's navel. Then cut the cord just beyond the clamp or knot on the *placental* side. Dip the end in antiseptic solution. Always soak your ties and instruments in antiseptic solution before use. If using ties, trim ends short, so that only a minimal amount of string remains around the umbilical stump.

Reviving the kitten: If the kitten isn't breathing, you'll have to cut the cord immediately so you can attempt to revive it. Rub the kitten briskly with a soft cloth and clear the secretions from its face. Suck excess fluids from the airway with an eyedropper or a small ear syringe. If that doesn't work, hold the kitten securely in both hands, firmly support the head so it doesn't flop, and sling the kitten upside down several times in a wide arc to force fluids from its respiratory passages. If the kitten still doesn't respond, blow tiny, gentle puffs of air into its mouth and nose and swing again. Once revived, warm the kitten by placing it next to a hot water bottle or on a heating pad.

Placentas: Throughout the delivery, count placentas carefully. There should be one delivered with or just after each kitten. A retained placenta can cause a serious postnatal infection. Also, never tug on the umbilical cord before the placenta is expelled completely. Doing so may tear the queen's uterus and cause life-threatening complications. Don't be alarmed if the queen eats the placentas, as this is her instinctive way of cleaning the nest so that predators won't be attracted by the birth odors. As soon as possible after delivery, remove the soiled towels from the kittening box and replace with clean, fresh bedding.

Trouble Signs

In most cases, the entire litter arrives within two to six hours. On rare occasions, a queen experiences a condition called *uterine inertia*, in which the contractions fade and the queen appears too tired to carry on even though there are obviously more kittens inside to be born. Seek medical advice if labor stops for more than two hours

between kittens, especially if the queen seems weak, listless, or restless.

If the queen bears down for an hour without producing a kitten, or if she partially delivers one and is obviously in distress, call a veterinarian or transport her to a clinic. Do not wait until she is too exhausted to deliver normally.

Kitten Development

Healthy kittens begin suckling just minutes after birth. It's important that they nurse right away so they can ingest disease-fighting antibodies contained in the mother's first milk, called the *colostrum*. Born with eyes and ears closed, each kitten selects its own nipple and seeks out the same teat each time to nurse.

If the kittens cry a lot and seem fretful, they may not be getting enough milk. Depending upon the problem, a veterinarian may be able to correct it by giving the queen a hormone injection to stimulate her milk flow.

After each meal, the mother licks the kittens' genitals to make them urinate and defecate. Should you ever find yourself faced with the grueling task of hand-raising and bottle-feeding kittens, you, too, will have to play Mom and stimulate elimination by massaging their tiny bottoms with a warm, damp wash cloth.

In about 10 days, the kittens' eyes begin to open. At first, all kittens' eyes are blue, changing to their adult shade at about 12 weeks of age. By 15 to 20 days old, kittens start crawling. Soon afterward, they begin to stand and toddle. It's important to note, however, that exotics tend to develop more slowly than some other breeds. From three weeks on, handle and play with the kittens daily. Experts say that kittens socialized to humans at an early age grow up to be better-adjusted, people-oriented pets. After four to six weeks, kittens can experiment with soft, solid cially formulated for growing kittens. By eight weeks, kittens should be weaned slowly and ready to receive their first shots. By 12 to 16 weeks, they can go to new homes.

A Breeder's Responsibility

Keep in mind that you will not make money breeding cats, after figuring in the total costs of showing, health care, stud fees, food, supplies, etc. You can, however, gain a great deal of satisfaction from knowing that you've helped create responsible cat owners by teaching buyers how to properly care for your kittens. When placing kittens, don't be afraid to interrogate potential buyers with questions such as:

• Do you intend to keep the new kitten indoors?
• Have you had cats before?
• Were they spayed or neutered?
• What did you feed them?
• Did they get annual medical care?
• What happened to them?
• Do you have other pets now?

Answers to these questions can reveal a lot about a person's attitude and knowledge about pet ownership. Because you decided to bring the kittens into the world, it is also your responsibility to make sure that each kitten goes to a home where it will be wanted, loved, and cared for. If you don't want the cat to be used for breeding, stipulate in a written contract that the individual registration form will not be released until you receive proof that the kitten has been spayed or neutered. Without this form, the new owner cannot register the kitten, nor can its future progeny be registered. Some cat-registering associations include space on their registration slips for breeders to indicate whether a cat can or cannot be used for breeding. If the "Not For Breeding" box is checked and signed, the association will not allow kittens from that cat to be registered.

Exotic youngsters grow into easygoing adults that make excellent companions.

foods. Also by this time, they can control their own elimination, and litter box training can begin. Raising kittens in a confined area keeps them safe, and also helps them toilet train faster.

At one month, kittens begin to play with each other, engaging in mock chase and combat games intended to hone their hunting skills.

To begin weaning, supplement mother's milk with meat varieties of jarred baby food (avoid those that contain onion) mixed with canned kitten milk replacer. A half-and-half mixture of canned, evaporated milk and water will also do, but avoid homogenized cow's milk. If refrigerated, warm milk to room temperature. At six weeks, start gradually replacing these supplements with a balanced, commercial cat food spe-

Useful Addresses and Literature

North American Cat Registries

American Association of Cat
  Enthusiasts (AACE)
P.O. Box 213
Pine Brook, NJ 07058
(201) 335-6717

American Cat Association (ACA)
8101 Katherine Avenue
Panorama City, CA 91402
(818) 781-5656

American Cat Fanciers Association
  (ACFA)
P.O. Box 203
Point Lookout, MO 65726
(417) 334-5430

Canadian Cat Association (CCA)
220 Advance Boulevard, Suite 101
Brampton, Ontario
Canada L6T 4J5
(905) 459-1481

Cat Fanciers' Association (CFA)
1805 Atlantic Avenue
P.O. Box 1005
Manasquan, NJ 08736-0805
(908) 528-9797

Cat Fanciers' Federation (CFF)
Box 661
Gratis, OH 45330
(513) 787-9009

National Cat Fanciers' Association
  (NCFA)
20305 West Burt Road
Brant, MI 48614
(517) 585-3179

The International Cat Association
  (TICA)
P.O. Box 2684
Harlingen, TX 78551
(210) 428-8046

United Feline Organization (UFO)
P.O. Box 3234
Olympia, WA 98509-3234
(360) 438-6903

Other Associations

American Humane Society
P.O. Box 1266
Denver, CO 80201
(303) 695-0811

American Society for the Prevention of
  Cruelty to Animals (ASPCA)
424 East 92nd Street
New York, NY 10128
(212) 876-7700

Cornell Feline Health Center
Cornell University College of
  Veterinary Medicine
Ithaca, NY 14853
(607) 253-3414

The Delta Society
P.O. Box 1080
Renton, WA 98057
(206) 226-7357

The Humane Society of the United
  States (HSUS)
2100 L Street, NW
Washington, DC 20037
(202) 452-1100

Morris Animal Foundation
45 Inverness Drive, East
Englewood, CO 80112-5480
(800) 243-2345

Pet Protection Services
TATOO-A-PET
6571 S.W. 20th Court
Fort Lauderdale, FL 33317
Hotline: (800) 828-8667
Office: (954) 581-5834

National Dog Registry
P.O. Box 116
Woodstock, NY 12498
Hotline: (800) 637-3547
Office: (914) 679-2355

Cat Magazines
CATS Magazine
Subscriptions:
P.O. Box 420240
Palm Coast, FL 32142-0240
(904) 445-2818
Editorial offices:
P.O. Box 290037
Port Orange, FL 32129-0037
(904) 788-2770

Cat Fancy
Subscriptions:
P.O. Box 52864
Boulder, CO 80322-2864
(303) 666-8504
Editorial offices:
P.O. Box 6050
Mission Viejo, CA 92690
(714) 855-8822

Cat Fancier's Almanac
Cat Fanciers' Association
1805 Atlantic Avenue
P.O. Box 1005
Manasquan, NJ 08736-0805
(908) 528-9797

Catnip (newsletter)
Tufts University School of Veterinary
   Medicine
Subscriptions:
P.O. Box 420014

Palm Coast, FL 32142-0014
(800) 829-0926
Editorial offices:
300 Atlantic Street, 10th Floor
Stamford, CT 06901
(203) 353-6650

Books
Behrend, Katrin and Wegler, Monika. *The Complete Book of Cat Care*. Hauppauge, New York: Barron's Educational Series, Inc., 1991.

Carlson, Delbert G., D.V.M., and Giffin, James M., M.D. *Cat Owner's Veterinary Handbook*. New York: Howell Book House, 1983.

Robinson, Roy. *Genetics for Cat Breeders*, 3rd ed. Oxford: Pergamon Press, 1991.

Siegal, Mordecai and Cornell University. *The Cornell Book of Cats*. New York: Villard Books, 1989.

Taylor, David. *The Ultimate Cat Book*. New York: Simon and Schuster, 1989.

Taylor, David. *You & Your Cat: A Complete Guide to the Health, Care & Behavior of Cats*. New York: Alfred A. Knopf, 1986.

Whiteley, H. Ellen, D.V.M. *Understanding and Training Your Cat or Kitten*. New York: Crown Trade Paperbacks, 1994.

Wright, Michael and Walters, Sally, eds. *The Book of the Cat*. New York: Summit Books, 1980.

Additional Reading
"Providing For Your Pets in the Event of Your Death or Hospitalization,"

Association of the Bar of the
   City of New York
Office of Communications
42 West 44th Street
New York, NY 10036-6690
   $2.00 per brochure. Enclose self-addressed, stamped envelope. To confirm immediate availability, call (212) 382-6695.

Index

Acclimation, 20–32
  arrival, 20
  supplies, 20–24
  to babies, 29
  to children, 28
  to other pets, 27
  training, 23, 31, 55
Acquisition, 11–19
  breeder, locating, 16
  housing considerations, 15
  kitten or adult, 12
  lifestyle considerations, 15
  price, 11
  questions to ask, 17
  registration, 18
  sales contract, 18
  second cat, 12
  selection, 17
AIDS, 50
Alcohol, 30, 41
Alleles, 95
Allergies, 54–55
  to cats, 12
Antifreeze, 26
Associations, 74

Bathing, 70
Beds, 22
Behavior:
  body language, 59
  hunting, 64
  scent marking, 65
  sexual, 93
  spraying, 65
  territorial, 65
  vocal communication, 59
Birth, 97–99
  complications, 92, 99
  equipment needed, 97
  labor, 97
  placentas, 99
  umbilical cord, 98
Boarding, 79
Breed standard, 80–90

Breeder-quality, 11
Breeding, 91–96
  problems, 92
  queen, selection, 91
  strategies, 96
  stud service, 92

Canned foods, 35
Cat carriers, 20, 78
Cat clubs, 74
Catnip, 24
Cat-proofing the house, 25–27
Cat shows, 73
Chocolate, 29, 41
Christmas trees, 30
Clawing, 66
Coat, shorthair, 7
  care of, 67
  colors, 81–90
Collars, 32
Colors, 81–90
Crossbreeding, 96

Declawing, 66
Dental care, 55
Diseases, 45–50
  calcivirus (FCV), 48
  chlamydiosis, 48
  distemper, 48
  gingivitis, 55
  herpes virus, 45
  immune deficiency virus (FIV), 50
  infectious peritonitis (FIP), 49
  leukemia virus (FeLV), 48
  lower urinary tract disease (LUTD), 36, 50
  panleukopenia virus, 48
  parasites, 51–54
  periodontal disease, 55
  pneumonitis, 48
  rabies, 49
  roundworms, 51
  tapeworms, 51

  viral rhinotracheitis (FVR), 45
Disqualify for show, 81
Distemper, 48
DNA, 95
Drowning, 26
Dry foods, 35

Ears, hearing, 61
  care, cleaning, 71
  mites, 54
Euthanasia, 58
Exotic Shorthair breed, origin of, 6
Eyes, 42, 60

Feeding, 33–41
  See also Food, Nutrition
Feline:
  calcivirus (FCV), 48
  immune deficiency virus (FIV), 50
  infectious peritonitis (FIP), 49
  leukemia virus (FeLV), 48
  panleukopenia virus (FPV), 48
  pneumonitis, 48
  urologic syndrome (FUS), 36, 50
  viral rhinotracheitis (FVR), 45
First aid, 46
Flea allergy dermatitis, 54
Fleas, 52
Flehmen response, 61
Food:
  adult maintenance, 34
  canned, 35
  dishes, 20
  dry, 35
  dry weight analysis, 38
  dog chow, 40
  guaranteed analysis, 37
  kitten, 33
  labels, 37
  premium quality, 35
  semimoist, 35
  senior cats, 34

Gender, 96
Genes, 7, 95
Genetics, 7, 95
  alleles, 95
  breeding, basics, 91–96
  chromosomes, 95
  coat colors, 95
  dominant genes, 7, 95
  heterozygous, 8
  homozygous, 8
  recessive genes, 7, 95
Gingivitis, 55
Grass, eating, 58
Grooming, 67–72
  bathing, 70–71
  supplies, 22, 70
  mats, removing, 69
Guaranteed analysis, 37

Hair balls, 57
Hazards, 25–27
  alcohol, 30, 41
  appliances, 25, 26
  chocolate, 29, 41
  holiday, 29
  in the home, 25
  outdoors, 30
  pools, ponds, 25
  windows, 25
Health care, 42–58
Heat cycle, 93
Heat stroke, 47
Homemade diets, 39
Hookworms, 51
House plants, 27
Hunting, 64
Hydrophobia:
  see Rabies, 49

Illnesses, 45–51
Immunizations, 44
Inbreeding, 96
Indoor vs. outdoor, 30
Induced ovulation, 94
Infectious diseases, 45–51

Jacobson's organ, 61

Kittens:
  birth, 97–99
  development of, 99
  food, 33

newborns, care of, 99
resuscitation of, 98
socialization of, 99

Leash training, 31
Linebreeding, 96
Litter boxes, 21
  problems, 62–63
Lower urinary tract disease
  (LUTD), 36, 50

Mating, 94
Medicating, 56
Microchip ID, 32
Milk, 39
Mites, 54
Multicat households, 63

Nail care, 72
Neonatal Isoerythrolysis (NI),
  92
Neutering, 13–14
Nutrition, 33–41
  AAFCO guidelines, 37
  life-cycle, 33

Obesity, 39
Outcrossing, 96

Parasites, 51–54
Periodontal disease, 55
Pet identification, 55
Pet theft, 31
Pet-quality, 11
Plants, poisonous, 26
Poison Control hotline, 47
Poisonings, accidental, 47
Pregnancy, 94
Purring, 60

Queen:
  breeding, age, 92
  heat cycles, 93
  selection, 91

Rabies, 39
Registration, 18
Restraint, 46
Righting reflex, 61
Ringworm, 54
Roundworms, 51
Rubbing, 65

Senses, 60
  Hearing, 61
  Sight, 60
  Smell, 61
  Taste, 61
  Touch, 61
Scent marking, 65
Scratching, 22–24
  behaviors, 22
  posts, 22–24
  problems, 22–24
Semimoist foods, 35
Sexing kittens, 13–14
Sexual behavior, 93–94
Shedding, 67
Showing, 73–79
Show-quality, 11
Show standard, 80–90
Skin problems, 54
Spaying, 13–14
Spraying, 65
Strings, dangers of, 24

Tapeworms, 51
Tattooing, 31
Taurine, 39
Tearing, excessive, 42
Teeth, brushing, 55
Temperament, 10
Territorial behavior,
  65–66
Ticks, 54
Toxoplasmosis, 29
Toys, 24
Travel by air, 78
Travel by car, 77

Urinary spraying, 65
Urinary tract health, 36, 50

Vaccinations, 44
Vegetarian diets, 39
Veterinarian:
  selection, 43
  when to call, 43
Vital signs, 58
Vocal communication, 59
Vomeronasal organ, 61

Water, 39
Window perches, 24
Window screens, 25